Taking Root
in
Provence

Taking Root
in
Provence

Anne-Marie Simons

Distinction Press
Waitsfield, Vermont

Taking Root in Provence
Anne-Marie Simons

Published by Distinction Press, LLC
354 Hastings Rd, Waitsfield, Vermont 05673
www.distinctionpress.com

Cover design and layout by Kitty Werner, RSBPress, LLC

Cover art and illustrations by Pierre Grenier,
    Aix-en-Provence, France, www. pierregrenier.net

ISBN: 978-0-9802175-7-5

Living well is the best revenge

— George Herbert

For Oscar, my fellow traveler

Aix-en-Provence

Ville d'eaux, Ville d'art says the brochure, the *waters* referring to the city's numerous fountains fed by the thermal springs that led Roman consul Gaius Sextius to establish a garrison here around 120 BC and creating the origins of Aquae Sextiae (Waters of Sextius), today's Aix-en-Provence.

The Dolphin

Celebrated throughout history as a friendly companion to humans, the dolphin is a symbol of joy, intelligence and freedom, while in medieval Christian art he was depicted as the guider of souls to paradise. The Dauphin of France used the dolphin as his icon for protection of his fleet and salvation for his country. Well represented in the city of Aix-en-Provence, the dolphin frolics happily in many of the city's fountains.

Contents

Introduction

When retirement came our way—a bit earlier than expected—my first reaction was: "Now I can travel." And perhaps write about it, I thought, this time without the limitations and deadlines of journalism. I have always been a bit of a gypsy and even though my origins lie in Holland, I have spent but a small part of my life there and have nowhere else grown roots so deep that it would have hurt me to pull them up. Heaven has sent me a soul mate just as un-"rooted" as I am and with an open mind as to our next address, so we decided to pull up stakes and see what happens.

The traveling continues, but this time from a new home base, and the writing—well, the longer we lived here the more I felt that this new life, this country, and our transition from fast-paced America to the slower-paced south of France, from one culture to another, is what I should write about. It took ten years, because it takes many experiences, some effort, and a lot of time to become fully integrated into this new world of our choice and to come to feel as "one of them." We have come to that point and I have lived (very happily) to tell about it.

The stories that follow relate some of the experiences, impressions, and observations from those first ten years, and give an idea of the cultural and natural richness of this area. It is a travelogue of sorts, and I hope that it will appeal to the armchair traveler or the tourist who comes to Provence. But it is also a look at everyday life among the French from my particular perch in Aix-en-Provence, which, even after ten years, remains my favorite place in the world.

Aix-en-Provence
August 2008

N.B. Many of the stories in this book have appeared in an earlier version, *Ten Years in Provence*, which was published in 2008. This expanded edition contains many new stories, additional recipes, and a renewed conviction that the pleasures and paradoxes of life in these parts continue to make Provence a very special place, indeed.

I think I could take root here.

Aix-en-Provence, 2011

Why Provence?

The world is a big place, but when you are looking to settle down somewhere—and this time without work-related constraints—you tend to quickly eliminate certain countries because they are too remote or too cold or too unstable or too foreign from your own culture, and pretty soon you realize that the world is not so big after all.

Early retirement allowed us to anticipate another twenty-five to thirty years of life, so why not look for a pleasant place to make the best of what was left? Our natural inclination directed us toward southern Europe (France, Italy, Spain) and a point-by-point comparison led to France. Not so much because we were sure that this was the best of all possible worlds, but because we felt it was worth a try. If it turned out to be disappointing we could always make another choice.

Culture, pleasant climate, natural beauty and easy access to international travel were all "conditions" in our search, but above all we looked for quality of life— seemingly simple, yet so hard to find, especially in the richer countries where money buys a certain level of comfort that might be confused with quality of life but often fails to provide that most important ingredient of all: freedom of worry.

We found it in Provence where all our conditions were met, and then some. Passing up the pleasures and burdens of the countryside, we looked for a city and chose Aix-en-Provence. This small city is more sophisticated than we expected, more international in scope, and rich in culture—the world-class Opera Festival alone worth the price of admission. Being half an hour away from the Mediterranean is an added benefit, as is the relaxed pace of the place. This is the slow lane, all the better to enjoy the beauty and pleasures that surround you, such as the daily markets where Oscar does his hunting and gathering every morning, or the mills where we buy our olive oil and the chateaux where we buy our wine.

One unexpected gift was the discovery of the French national health system, which some people have called a model to the world. Health care is considered a right, not a privilege, and should be accessible and affordable to all. The French *Sécurité Sociale* makes sure that it is. As foreign residents in this country with American health insurance, we have both had the "pleasure" to compare the two systems in minor and major ways, and have nothing but praise for what we found: excellent care at a fraction of the cost we used to pay, and doctors who still make house calls! Prescription drugs are often so inexpensive that we do not bother to send in our bills for partial reimbursement. This, too, is quality of life.

One day we had a car accident here when a distracted driver ran into us. He immediately admitted it was his fault, but in a reflexive gesture I flagged down a passing gendarme expecting him to write an accident report for our insurance. "Is anybody hurt?" he asked, and when I answered "No," he said *"Alors?..."* and got back on his motorcycle. In a collision such as ours (more than a simple fender bender, two doors to be replaced), the two drivers concerned simply complete an insurance form (to be carried in every car), agree on the facts and sign. The insurance companies do the rest. Our car got repaired and I never saw a bill. No need for lawyers.

My French friends react with surprise when I marvel at all of this. *"C'est normal,"* they say, and of course it is. It's just one more of those things (like affordable education and health care) that enhance the quality of life in these parts and that are totally taken for granted.

Sometimes the French don't seem to know how good they have it, but—keep it under your hat—we do. More than ten years after settling here, fluent in the ways of the locals and with a French driver's license in our wallet, we can confidently say that our choice of Aix-en-Provence was the right one. We are definitely *chez nous.*

Cooking Secrets

Food is important in this country and everybody cooks well, men and women alike. All social life takes place around the table, where one talks about food above all else. Recipes are exchanged, addresses offered, and recommendations made. It soon becomes apparent that not all market stalls are alike, not all farmers sell home-grown produce, and not all truffle vendors are honest. Of course, restaurants are not forgotten and recent discoveries are either praised or viciously attacked.

In asking for advice it is important, however, to consider the source. For example, a Parisian friend with a house in this area responded to our request for restaurant suggestions by saying, "In Aix? *On ne mange pas à Aix.*" (One doesn't eat in Aix). A bit severe, we thought.

Food debate is not limited to the dinner table, and it is not uncommon to overhear discussions like this one at the markets: "Potatoes in *brandade de morue*? *Jamais de la vie, Monsieur!* Oh, your mother did? Where are you from? Alsace? Well, perhaps they do over there, but not in Provence. No sir! Just make sure you use a good olive oil. Now, what are you going to serve with that? *Soupe au pistou*? Excellent idea. You'll want the three kinds of beans, onions, basil, carrots and tomatoes, this, that and the other..." while the other customers not only patiently wait but begin to participate. "You may also want to add courgettes, monsieur" says a woman in line. "And make sure you add lots of garlic," says another. "My wife doesn't like garlic but she doubles the parmesan cheese at the end" says a man. "*Curieux*," says another with eyebrows raised. And so goes the daily market...

The fishmonger never fails to ask you how you plan to prepare your fish. Broil or barbecue? He won't scale them. In the oven? He'll give you extra fennel. Not sure? He'll make a recommendation and insists you tell him the next day how it was. To the cat owner he'll give fish heads, to little old pensioners an extra free portion. To all, his non-stop cheery chatter from behind the counter which is piled high with finned or shelled or tentacled sea life on ice and half a swordfish whose sharp sword is blunted with a lemon.

When it comes to cooking, advice is plentiful and everybody is willing to part with some. One day, our mason Charlie, a seventy-year old authentic Provençal who built our *cave* in the dark, vaulted, seventeenth-century dungeon that is our basement, shared with us his mother's secret for preparing snails—the ordinary garden variety that he collects by the bucketful after a rainstorm. The trick, said Charlie, is that you have to tire them before cooking. Yep... *il faut fatiguer les escargots!* He then showed Oscar how to stroke them one by one to coax their head out of the shell and re-lax them. Then you drop them in lukewarm water and bring them slowly to a boil. Never throw them in boiling water because that makes them tighten up and harden. I suspect that restaurant chefs dispense with the stroking, but I do admit that Charlie's snails are among the best I have ever tasted.

This reminds me of the elderly mother of my friend Gaby who had similar convictions. After putting the *escargots* in lukewarm water she would talk to them and say *"Je vais à la Messe maintenant"* (I am going to church now) before putting the lid on the pot and turning up the heat. Let's hope their last memories were pleasant: a good massage, a lukewarm bath, a soft voice in your ear—and sleep.

A Long Hot Summer

Summer in Provence means hot and dry weather, which is not unpleasant unless there is a *canicule*—a heat wave. You may remember the awful heat wave of 2003 that killed some fifteen thousand people in France, most of them elderly and living alone in Paris. For four long months we had temperatures of thirty to thirty-five degrees Celsius every day, and hospitals (understaffed in summer) were overrun by patients with heatstroke or dehydration. Granted, the circumstances were extreme but they revealed some major weaknesses in emergency response and cost the minister of health his job.

At times like that, we city dwellers live like moles in our darkened, non-air-conditioned apartments, windows and shutters closed from morning to evening, and carefully choosing our outings based on the presence of air-conditioning (department store, bookstore, movie theater or—for the ultimate cooldown—Picard, the frozen-food specialist, where a brief walk through the aisles is guaranteed to bring down your body temperature to winter levels). Movie theaters, by the way, are not only air-conditioned but have very comfortable seats with headrests, so if the movie is no good you do a siesta. The only people you will meet there in the afternoons are retirees who are probably there for the same reason as you.

From time to time, we may visit friends in the countryside who generously share their pools with apartment dwellers like us. The formula is simple: you bring something to be grilled for lunch (mostly fish like sardines or calamari or *dorade*, bought that morning at the market), share a salad or whatever is available, drink rosé wine, take a swim every so often and find a shady spot for a nap. A great way to get through a hot summer day.

Others rush like lemmings to the sea but the beach is not our favorite place, especially not in summer when tourists take over the entire coast. Luckily, friends in the know have introduced us to some uncharted little beaches near Marseilles, where we meet in late afternoon when the few local families take their last swim and go home. There, in the crystal-clear water of a *calanque* (fjord-like inlet) we swim and snorkel all alone until sunset, incredulous that not ten miles away people fight for a speck of beach and stand in line for a sandwich. Once the sun sets, we prepare a picnic or go to a nearby restaurant for a seafood dinner. Our favorite is called *Le Lunch* but serves dinner, which nobody seems to find unusual.

Somehow, this fits Marseilles and its Marcel Pagnol characters. The city's motto: *Doucement le matin, pas trop vite le soir* (Slowly in the morning, not too fast in the evening) is a good indication of the laid-back attitude of the Marseillais who are well aware of their privileged surroundings and mean to enjoy them to the fullest. The pace of Paris is not for them; a bit of fishing, perhaps a little boat, and a pastis at a favorite bar in the *Vieux Port* is all they need to be happy.

But this hot summer the picture was clouded by an unwelcome incident. For three weeks in June, newspapers and television reported breathlessly about a black panther that had been seen in the Calanques, a nature reserve between Marseilles and Cassis noted for its crystalline inlets and secluded little beaches that are only accessible from the sea or by hiking through pine forests and down steep cliffs. This area is particularly beloved by the local people of the region who come to swim and picnic here, far from the tourist crowds. So they were not happy when the mayors of Marseilles and Cassis decided to close the eleven-hundred-hectare Calanques area, including the beaches, after a black panther had been spotted. For good measure, policemen and gendarmes were posted at all the access roads, and signs put up that said "Closed due to presence of animal presumed dangerous."

This being France, numerous meetings were then held where numerous solutions were proposed and rejected, including the one of a massive safari by the army. When everyone had had his say—the police, gendarmerie, fire brigade, and national bureau of the hunt—a grid map of the area was drawn up and covered on foot and in SUV's by one hundred fifty members of all afore-mentioned groups. To no avail. They collected footprints and droppings but no panther. The droppings and footprint casts were sent to the *Office National de la Chasse et de la Faune Sauvage* for study while the locals boiled. After three weeks of deprivation they wanted their calanques back and threatened to take matters into their own hands. That was when the news broke. Banner headlines in the newspaper announced that the black panther was found to be...a cat! A big cat, all right, but a cat nevertheless. Embarrassed officials ordered the calanques re-opened immediately and prepared for the ridicule that was soon to follow: "The black panther joins the giant sardine in Marseilles!" was one of the headlines, dredging up the "Sardine blocks port of Marseilles" story that had appeared years ago when a fishing boat called La Sardine sank at the entry of the old port of Marseilles and effectively blocked it. Who says you can't believe what you read in the papers?

Markets and Rentrée

In September our markets return to normal. With fewer tourists, the vendors have time again to discuss recipes, the weather, and the pros and cons of zucchini in *soupe au pistou*. Our old cheese maker, who has been promising us a *cachaille* for years now, is back and again greets Oscar with a wide grin and *"Je n'ai pas oublié, Monsieur!"* but still no *cachaille*… (*Cachaille* is a smelly paste made of hard dry pieces of goat cheese that for many weeks have been softened and ripened in a combination of olive oil, garlic and grappa. It makes your eyes water and your papilla panic, but must be tried at least once.) The little old lady is still there who sells eggs and live fowl, each egg to be individually wrapped in newspaper and the guinea fowl in a little cage with the price marked as "€8 the pair." It seems fitting that the pair is not split up for their final trip— together until death do them part.

Sadly, Annamaria did not return this year and rumor has it that she is very sick and should not be expected back. This lively, good-looking Italian wife of a French farmer liked to discuss recipes with Oscar once they had discovered a common origin in their mothers' backgrounds (Italian-Croatian) and hence a similar way of preparing certain dishes. Faina (farinata), torta pasqualina, risotto, milanesas—it's all the same thing whether made in Italy or Argentina.

Mrs. F. is again at her usual table in the Happy Days bar, where her daughter Monique parks her every morning for an hour while she does her marketing. The waiters all know the ninety-two-year-old lady and watch over her protectively until Monique returns and mother and daughter have a pastis together before they slowly walk back to their nearby apartment.

The best home-made jams are still to be found at the stall of the *Petites Soeurs de Jésus* (a local order of nuns who do a killer business with their preserves, vegetables and field flowers), and our Parisian friends complain only slightly less about the throngs of tourists (half of whom are Parisian) at the village markets, where more and more trinkets and gadgets are crowding out the local farm produce.

The North Africans are there again with their tables of colorful spices presented in little cloth-lined baskets, their heaps of dried rosebuds, and their sacks of semolina for couscous. I always worry about the weather when I see the finer powders (like turmeric) exposed to a potential *coup de mistral*, but so far no natural disaster has occurred. A neighboring vendor carries a large variety of olives, chickpeas, hummus, pita bread, and home-made spicy condiments like the fire-hot *harissa*.

This is the beginning of mushroom season and long tables stacked with mounds of different mushrooms begin to appear in the markets. I have never known such a variety of *champignons: chanterelles, cèpes, girolles, pieds de mouton, trompettes de la mort* (bon appétit!), *lactaires, morilles, mousserons,* and more. Sautéed in olive oil with parsley and garlic, it is one of the seasonal pleasures of the table, and a promising prelude to the truffle season which is still a couple of months off.

———•———

September is also *La Rentrée* in France. Return to school, to politics after a blessedly quiet summer, and even to literature. For at least a week, *La Rentrée Scolaire* is the lead story on television. Even though nothing ever changes (crying children, anxious mothers, etc.), in early September *La Rentrée* displaces war, forest fires, and even strikes. As for *La Rentrée Littéraire*, when publishers introduce their new books and new authors, this year looks only slightly more encouraging than an earlier *Rentrée* when most of the seven hundred new titles could be filed under the heading "Libido, my Libido"—to give you an idea of that year's trend. Many of these books were written by sour-looking youngsters or by pseudo intellectuals who invite us to crawl into their beds and partake of their sex lives which, they seem to think, is really worth knowing about. Among the bestsellers, for example, was "*La Vie Sexuelle de Catherine M*"—whose author appears to be in her fifties and is interviewed on television talk shows (sometimes with her husband) where serious-looking hosts address her reverentially and nobody cracks a smile. Two of last year's new books were written by thirteen- and sixteen-year old girls who—if the critics are to be believed—are definitely not the next Françoise Sagan. Back to school for them. Publishing isn't what it used to be, not even in France where I thought literature fared better than most anywhere else.

Draught Horses and Donkeys

The village of Villelaure, about 40 km. from Aix-en-Provence, celebrates the *Fête de la Traction Animale et de la Transhumance* in early September. If you admire horsepower in the raw, this is your event. Among the highlights was a demonstration of draught horses at work, pulling a plow and making a perfect furrow, or simply showing their form by trotting by the stands and providing a close view of their humongous hulk. I never thought I would see beauty in mere mass, but to see one ton of muscle up close is very convincing. The horses were introduced by name and weight: "On the outside, Titus, a Breton of one thousand kilos; next to him Hannibal, a Percheron of eleven hundred kilos," etc. I learned about Pioles, Ardennais, Comtois and many other draught horses, and couldn't help being impressed. There is something very quiet and accepting about them, always pulling one thing or another and never being aggressive or brusque. If it didn't sound so puny, I would call them sweet.

The *Fête* started with a parade of all the animals that would later on participate in demonstrations or games. To begin with, there were the *Charretiers du Luberon* who showed off their horses and wagons—

jardinières or fjords or six-in-hand—sometimes stocked with chickens or goats to take to market. There were donkeys and goats pulling children's carts (Provençal donkeys with huge ears). There were the *Gardians de la Camargue*, the cowboys from the Camargue area on their white horses, carrying long cattle prods. There were lots of goats, a pig the size of a cow, and a huge flock of sheep. The sheep were part of the *Transhumance*, the estival movement of sheep and goats into the mountains and back down again. We had already seen these flocks during our trips through the countryside but did not realize that this is not a folkloric phenomenon but an economic and ecological one. The sheep not only feed well in higher elevations but keep the fire hazard down by eating dry shrub and are part of the ecological balance. The flock in Villelaure had just come down from the mountain with their shepherd, a few dogs and a couple of goats. (Apparently, there are often a few she-goats in a flock of sheep because they help nurse the lambs).

There was a marching band in Napoleonic dress with white-plumed hats, and a folkloric dance group with fife and drums that sang the *Coupo Santo*, the hymn of Provence, in the Langue d'Oc (similar to Catalan). The entire parade ended in the town square, where music and dances were performed. Then lunch was served for six hundred people. For €10 we ate Aïoli (codfish with boiled vegetables, chickpeas and pota-toes, accompanied by a strong garlic mayonnaise), cheese, fruit and coffee and, of course, wine *à volonté*. We sat at long tables under the plane trees and had a lively discussion with some Parisians about the importance of tradition and folklore.

After lunch we all moved to a huge field where the *Nacioun Gardiano* (the Camargue cowboys) demonstrated their horsemanship and did some medieval games where a horseman in full gallop had to put his lance through a small ring that dangled from a pole or where he had to conquer a small bouquet of flowers from another horseman and give it to his beloved *Arlésienne*. During some of this chivalrous activity, I heard a soft snoring next to me in the grass and found that Oscar, full of aïoli and wine and happy thoughts, was taking a post-prandial nap. Only when the big draught horses came by, six abreast, in a gentle trot that made the earth shake, did he wake up. The announcer had just mentioned that a local farmer collected these draught horses as a hobby, the way other people collect silver spoons. *"Mais ce n'est pas des petites cuillères d'argent, ça!"* he said admiringly.

The grand finale of the day was the donkey stunt. This had been billed as an attempt at harnessing forty donkeys to make them pull a hay wagon. I appreciated the "attempt" when I saw what it took to make forty stubborn asses all do the same thing at the same time. It wasn't easy and took a long time, but it finally worked. A world record, according to the announcer.

Happy and smelly, reeking of garlic and animal droppings, we finally drove back to "civilization" and a hot bath. At times like these, Washington seems a distant memory, indeed.

Hikes and Picnics

In this relaxed environment of southern France I see less evidence of sports activity than in the United States. Fewer sports clubs, it seems (except for young athletes), but more spas and fitness centers. Our set (let's say over fifty) will sail or swim, but jogging is considered the domain of the young. "Running? Only in flight or in pursuit!" as Jonathan Miller said.

When we first arrived here from Washington, D.C., we had fond memories of the miles of trails through Rock Creek Park and of the bike path along the C&O Canal from Georgetown into Maryland which on weekends would fairly vibrate with hard-breathing exercisers. We bicycled to Mount Vernon, jogged to the Mall to watch a Sunday-afternoon polo match, or to the zoo to watch the pandas. But when we unpacked our bikes on arrival in Aix-en-Provence, we soon realized that Aix isn't Washington and that here, in the old city center, there is no open space, no bike path, and no place to store our bikes at home.

So hiking seemed the way to go and as luck would have it, *everybody* hikes. Weather permitting, Sundays are set aside for long walks in one of the many wild or protected natural parks in the area—the mountainous

Luberon with its Gorges du Régalon, the Alpilles and the bald-topped Mont Ventoux, the more verdant Contadour with its hundred-year-old dry-stone *bergeries* (refuges) where you can spend the night, the narrow paths overlooking the *calanques* near Marseilles or Cassis with their stupendous views, the Camargue before mosquitoes take it over, or the nature reservation on the island of Port Cros where no cars or even bicycles are allowed—the choice is rich and varied.

A nice by-product of hiking in France is that you are never far away from History. On a walk in the Vaucluse you may encounter the Mur de la Peste which was erected to keep the plague that had hit Marseilles in 1720 from spreading to other counties. Or on your way to the Montagne Sainte Victoire you may pass the Tour César, a fourteenth-century watch tower that overlooks a vast plateau and the city of Aix-en-Provence. From here, the view of the Sainte Victoire mountain may entice you to climb it one day up to the seventeenth-century Notre-Dame-de-Sainte-Victoire chapel and the Croix de Provence at just over one thousand meters (most recently restored in 1870 after two previous crosses had been blown down by the strong mistral winds). At the foot of the Montagne Sainte Victoire you may come across the remains of the Oppidum d'Untinos, a Celto-Ligurian settlement dating from the third century B.C. that survived dispersement by the Romans until the eleventh century. Provence counts three Cistercian abbeys, all open to the public and well worth a visit, and all surrounded by beautiful, walkable countryside. The Massif de la Sainte-Baume has a marked trail that leads to the grotto where Mary Magdalene is believed to have lived until her death. Pilgrimage to the site can be traced back to the fifth century and Mary Magdalene's sarcophagus can be seen today in the Basilique Sainte-Marie-Madeleine in nearby St. Maximin, center of early Christianity in Provence.

These historical facts add interest to some of our walks, but we walk mainly for exercise. So after some timid tryouts on our own, we ventured out with some friends who not only are experienced hikers but who know all the best places, and soon the Sunday-walk-with-friends had become a regular part of our weekends. At Easter time we pick wild asparagus and onions; in the fall we collect mushrooms; we bring home wild thyme and rosemary, and sometimes an interesting rock for an artist friend. And of course there is no such thing as a hike without a picnic.

Not surprisingly, a French picnic is not a simple sandwich. Not even a delicious, multi-layered super sandwich. The idea is that everyone brings what he eats, including a baguette, but by the time we sit down and pull out our various meals the sharing begins as the first Tupperware is passed around. This can be olives or crudités or pâté; perhaps fried zucchini flowers or tabouleh salad; often a sausage, or cold chicken, or the leftovers of a savory *daube* (stew) or roast; various cheeses, fruit and some chocolate bars. Though we all carry at least one liter of water each in our canteen, there is always a bottle of red wine to pass around, and inevitably the talk that accompanies the meal is about food and cooking.

Some of us then stretch out for a snooze in the shade, heads resting on our backpacks, while others whisper on for a while, or use their binoculars to scan the landscape or to try to detect a lizard on a nearby old wall. The silence is broken only by the distant calling of a bird or the buzzing of a fly or a soft snoring in the grass. Peace and contentment reign—until the snorers stir into consciousness and it is time to brush off the grass and dirt and take to the road again.

We usually walk three hours before lunch and two to three hours after, ending our outing at a café for a *panaché* or a hot chocolate. As we get ready to head home with our wild thyme and rosemary a last bit of advice accompanies us to our car: remember the thyme ice cream I told you about!

On the way home we pass clusters of vibrantly colored cyclists bent over their racing bikes as they whoosh through the countryside and down steep mountain roads in Tour de France mode. This is Sunday and this is France, and on a sunny Sunday afternoon the French countryside without cyclists is as unthinkable as Paris without the Eiffel tower.

Olive Festival in Mouriès

The village of Mouriès near Saint-Rémy de Provence is justly famous for its celebration in mid-September of the *Olives Vertes* or *Olives Cassées*. These are the crisp bright-green early olives, so named because their skin is slightly cracked to release any bitterness before they are immersed in fennel-flavored brine.

Since time immemorial this early olive harvest has been celebrated with the usual religious and pagan rituals, but the festivities in Mouriès have gone well beyond their modest origins and today comprise an impressive gathering of dozens of folkloristic groups from Marseilles, Avignon, Arles, Nîmes, Rodez, Toulon and as far away as Nice, all of them dressed in their local traditional costume. There were a surprising number of young people among these groups and they were not your typical farm boys either. One young man with dreadlocks and another with tattoos peeking out from under his costume seemed to indicate that tradition holds its place among the different generations.

After a Sunday-morning mass said in Provençal, and a blessing of the animals who never fail to leave their smelly heaps of testimony in front of the church steps, the gathered groups parade slowly through the little town, on foot or on horseback, on simple farmer's carts or in elaborate open coaches, walking or dancing to the music of the accompanying bands.

The first open coach drawn by six black Frisian horses was the one carrying the newly crowned Queen of Arles, accompanied by three notables. This new queen—*prima inter pares* among a dozen or so former queens—is beautifully dressed in the traditional Arlésienne costume of long silk dress, lace triangular shawl, small coif on an upswept hairdo, and little lace parasol. The long-sleeved dress has a small bustle and a short train and is very elegant. The Queen's maids of honor followed in another horse-drawn carriage, and four former queens in a third, while other Arlésiennes rode side-saddle on white horses from the Camargue and, finally, a large coterie on foot, sometimes with children in traditional dress, closed the Arlésiennes contingent.

Among the simpler folk was a group of olive pickers—men and women—in traditional working clothes and wooden shoes, pushing a cart with the three-legged ladder and woven baskets of their trade, and followed by a smaller cart carrying grandmother. There was a shepherd with some sheep shorn for the occasion in a pretty pattern, and of course the ever-present *Nacioun Gardiano* cowboys on their white Camargue horses that were decorated for the day with olive branches.

All texts on flags and banners were in Occitan, the language of Provence so similar to Catalan and still spoken widely in these villages. There even is a television news program in Provençal with subtitles in French. Frédéric Mistral, great defender of the Provençal language who received the Nobel Prize for literature in 1904, would be pleased. So would Alphonse Daudet who wrote his "Lettres de Mon Moulin" from a mill in these parts.

After two tours of the village the cortège dissolved around its reserved luncheon tables set up under the *platanes* of the school playground, while tourists and locals quickly invaded all available bar and restaurant space in town. Sunday lunch is a serious business and this one was amply complemented by a *dégustation* of local products, such as *olives cassées, fougasses* (flat fo-

caccia-type bread), honey-based cakes, and, of course, wine *à volonté*. A solid base for the afternoon activities which included a *Course Camarguaise* in the local arena.

Unlike the *corrida*, where bulls are killed, this *Course* is a game of skill and speed that leaves both animal and man undamaged. A fierce-looking bull from the Camargue faces a young man in tennis shoes who tries to grab one of several small items that have been placed on the bull's head, i.e., a rosette on the bull's forehead, two little white cloth balls on his ears, and a string tied around the base of each of his horns. These five items are called "attributes" and it is the task of the *raseteur*, the young man who holds a small comb (a *raset*) in his hand, to grab one of these items as the bull charges him with his head down. For each attribute the raseteur is awarded a sum of money put up by local sponsors, but he has to work fast because the bull stays in the arena for only fifteen minutes.

The raseteurs work in groups of ten or more, all dressed in long white pants, white T-shirts, and tennis shoes. Once the bull has had a minute to run around, snort, scrape the ground and otherwise acquaint himself with the arena, a signal is given and the raseteurs jump the barricade and run towards the bull who, disoriented, does not know which one to charge. Some "older" raseteurs then try to attract the bull with their shouts while a faster youngster runs across the bull's path and reaches between the horns to grab the rosette, after which he jumps the barricade in a flying leap. It does happen that the bull flies after him across the barricade, but accidents are rare. Meanwhile, a loudspeaker announces the prize money being contributed by the local butcher, bistro, hardware store, pharmacy, etc. and signals the end of each fifteen-minute *Course*. If the raseteurs did not manage to lift all the attributes off the bull's head, the bull may leave the arena with one or more strings still wrapped around his horns for which he gets applauded.

It's a daring game of speed and agility, played out in a packed arena where some Arlésiennes and other costumed locals can be spotted among the spectators. It's colorful and lively and fun. No blood in the sand here.

St. Tropez and Other Pleasures

Over the years, we have had the pleasure to be invited for a few days on a friend's sailboat for the *Voiles de St. Tropez*. This is an annual sailing regatta in the Bay of St. Tropez the first week of October, where boats of different categories—from beautiful wooden three-masters dating from the late 1800s to today's fiberglass models—compete for a week. It is a beautiful sight, those white sails and brightly colored spinnakers against blue skies and the pretty backdrop of St. Tropez village. And when the boats are all tied up in the small port, swabbed, buffed and polished, and jealously guarded by their crews in uniform, they look like so many beauty queens in a contest vying for the admiration of the crowds and the votes of the judges.

During the regatta, we had dropped anchor in front of La Madrague, Brigitte Bardot's house in a quiet cove, for a spot of lunch on deck and were surprised to have a small motorboat come alongside afterwards to ask if we had any garbage. How smart! The week of the regatta, the City of St. Tropez collects your wine bottles, plastic bags and other *déchets* in order to avoid heaps of garbage in and around the few trash bins in the port. In the evenings, the local bars were crawling with crews from New Zealand, Australia, England, Italy, Spain and elsewhere and it struck me that they were all good-looking. Healthy, rugged, tanned good looks on all of them—not a single nerdy type among them. The latter may have paid for the boat but they surely were not sailing her.

———♦———

Since we settled in Provence, we have attended numerous celebrations of one thing or another—saints, foods, animals, summer solstice, etc.—and we hope to keep doing so. But some of the old traditions are in trouble, as witnessed by this headline in the local newspaper: *"Avec la disparition du dernier berger, le pastoralisme menacé."* (Pastoralism in danger of disappearing after death of shepherd). In the village of Eguilles, the last shepherd died and there is nobody to take over. For the past eighteen years, this shepherd had been taking his flock of several thousand sheep up the mountain until he took a fatal fall there. The paper waxes nostalgic about the *transhumance*—the annual passage of the sheep through the village on their way to a mountain meadow, the shepherd in front with his staff, his shotgun and his small lantern, the flock flanked by a few sheepdogs, and all the villagers standing in their doorway to watch the passage which can take several hours. Today's young are not up to the task, and the lonely shepherd, who for all his solitude can barely make a living, is difficult to replace. Add to that the problem of wolves who at the insistence of the Green party have been re-introduced into the region— and who sometimes decimate the flocks—and you can see that the Transhumance may soon be a thing of the past. Another tradition lost. *Quel dommage!*

———•———

We finally gave in to the call of the local siren, *la Montagne Sainte Victoire* just outside Aix-en-Provence, revered by the locals and painted by Cézanne close to a hundred times. To scale this table-shaped mountain of just over three thousand feet (one thousand meters) seemed a nice Sunday activity and within our increasingly limited abilities. A guidebook of regional nature hikes indicated various ascents and we chose the shortest one, thinking a three-hour hike (from the four-hundred-meter level) would be a better start for us than a five-hour hike. We chose unwisely, as it turned out. The unforgiving logic of the shortest distance to the top meant the steepest and most direct way up. Less zigzagging, more climbing, more catching-our-breath stops, more dehydration and the panicky realization that we did not bring enough water.

When we finally got to the summit, we barely took the time to enjoy the splendid view, visit the seventeenth-century Chapel of *Notre-Dame-de-Sainte-Victoire* and take a brief cool-down rest at the refuge. We feared the waterless and difficult descent ahead of us and knew that darkness comes suddenly at this time of year. Well—we made it, but just barely, and have been aching all week. Another painful lesson in humility.

Where There is Smoke…

Our apartment in Aix-en-Provence was described as *d'époque* in the realtor's fact sheet, which meant that it dated from the eighteenth century, had high ceilings, and came with many of the original fixtures, such as the hexagonal floor tiles called *tomettes* and a wonderful marble fireplace in the bedroom. It was the fireplace that hooked us.

D'époque also meant that there were no built-in closets (people used armoires) and no elevator, but we decided that two flights of stairs would do us good and that we could build the missing closets. That accomplished, we called in the chimney sweeps to have our fireplace checked and prepared for winter. After two or three appointments that somehow came and went (you get used to this quickly), we watched with fascination as the sweeps first removed a wooden board and a layer of insulation that previous owners had installed to close off the chimney. Then they brought out what seemed like mountains of soot, which they carefully collected into large plastic garbage bags to be used, as they explained, for gardening. Next came the brushing and vacuuming of the chimney canal and a final inspection by flashlight, and we were declared operational, with a signed certificate to boot.

By late November the evenings turn chilly and we looked forward to building a nice fire—our first one—in the fireplace. We stacked the logs, lit some kindling, and sat back to watch the flames slowly licking their way up the logs. The smell, the crackling and the pretty glow cast into the room enveloped us in a cloud of well-being as we leaned back with a drink to enjoy the spectacle.

Not half an hour later, however, an urgent ringing of our doorbell broke the spell and we faced a worried-looking young girl who asked us if we had a fireplace. Affirmative. "You are smoking me out of my apartment," she said, pointing to a rooftop down the street. Concerned and uncomprehending, we followed her to a building two houses over, where she had rented a small walk-up apartment on the fifth and final floor. It was dense with smoke, which we saw pouring out from under the stairs that led to her sleeping loft. We were perplexed and told her we would immediately stop using our fireplace and investigate.

The chimney sweeps assured us that they had removed all obstructions until they had a clear view of the sky. With that, we called our old mason Charlie, who had built many fireplaces and renovated numerous old houses in his day and who was as intrigued as we were by the fact that our chimney smoke could somehow invade an apartment two houses away and several stories higher up. The next day he climbed up the roof of our four-story building with an agility belying his age and faced five chimneys. "Go get a pizza," he then instructed me. "Already thinking about lunch," I thought at first, but he continued, "and burn the box in your fireplace." I quickly learned that a greasy pizza box makes good white smoke which would help him to identify our chimney.

As he walked across the roof and checked our chimney I heard a triumphant "Ahaa!" and soon saw him coming down the steep ladder shaking his head. "*Incroyable*," he muttered, and asked us to follow him to the girl's apartment. There he found the proof he had been looking for as he showed us the "improvements" of an irresponsible landlord, who at one time had built an illegal addition on the roof of his building with one wall built against our chimney. Later, taking advantage of an ongoing shortage of student housing in Aix, he had added a mezzanine sleeping loft in this rooftop studio so he could rent it as a two-room apartment. He had simply installed a heavy wooden beam to support the sleeping floor and had anchored this beam into our chimney!

When confronted with our findings, the landlord simply said "I thought your chimney was unused," and assured us he was going to take care of the problem. We told him that we had already instructed our mason to do so and had contacted our insurance company in view of possible liability. That seemed to scare him and he complied dutifully thereafter. But a few weeks later when I saw his tenant in the street, she told me that the landlord had given her notice because he was selling the apartment.

Nowadays, as I walk through Aix I often look up at the rooftops where I spot many unsightly "improvements" and wonder how these could have escaped the building regulations in the historic center of town and how many renters may have been endangered like our young girl.

Truffles and Tricks

In November, the brighter colors slowly fade from our farmers' markets to make way for the more subdued tones of autumn produce: apples, pears, pumpkins, turnips, cabbage, endives, walnuts, quince, and litchis. The locally grown sunflowers are gone for another year and replaced by asters and mums. Soon, the smell of roasted chestnuts will waft over the Cours Mirabeau, and the food shop windows will fill up with *Cassoulet, Saucisse Lyonnaise, Tripes à la Catalane* and *Choucroute Garnie*, so you know winter is not far off.

Winter is announced by the arrival of truffles in late November or early December. Truffles can be bought from some farmers at our daily market, but going to a special truffle market, such as Aups, a ninety-minute drive from Aix-en-Provence, can be an interesting experience. On Thursday mornings during the season, restaurant owners and other big buyers go and buy their truffles in Aups. It's done by haggling and negotiating, and best done in Provençal. Few words are exchanged, and offers are made and countered on little pieces of paper. If the seller does not know you he will not sell to you because he is afraid you may be from the "Fisc" (the French IRS). It's a cash business—no checks or credit cards, and of course no receipts or records.

Once a year, this truffle market is held on a Sunday and opened to the public, and that day all truffle vendors in Aups sell at the same price. The price is indeed controlled but, sadly, not the quality. It was in Aups that we bought our one bad truffle, a Chinese one. Truffles vary in quality like any other natural product, but nature does not produce dirt-covered radishes that look and smell like truffles. China does. Unscrupulous truffle growers will buy these Chinese look-alikes and mix them with the real thing. After a short time of cohabitation, these phony ones will take on the smell of real truffles and be passed off for the authentic and expensive "black gold." There is no sure way to avoid a bad truffle, but we have found a perfect solution in the person of a restaurant owner who is willing to sell us, under the counter, the truffles he buys directly from a trusted farmer. He pays wholesale, we pay him retail, and everybody is happy.

Wild truffles were once plentiful here and reasonably priced. Many farmers and villagers would flavor their rustic fare with shaved or grated truffles and they valued the truffle no more than perhaps a good onion or other enhancer. But as the truffle harvest diminished over time (from one thousand tons per year a century ago to forty tons today) and phylloxera or drought dealt a severe blow to the already reduced crops, the truffle became the rare and high-priced commodity it is today.

Our local black truffle is of the *Tuber Melanosporum* variety, a delicacy known since Greek and Roman times. It grows at the base of certain trees (mostly oak) in limestone soil. To locate them, farmers have traditionally used female pigs but are increasingly switching to small dogs who are more willing to give up their trophies than pigs. Female pigs have an inborn instinct to find truffles because these apparently smell like the male pig's sex scent, but the pig will eat the truffle as soon as it digs it up and only quick action on the part of the farmer will snatch his black gold from the pig's jaws. Therefore, certain dogs are preferred these days but they need to be trained and not all dogs are good students.

It is hard to see black gold in the warty grayish-black lump that is the French truffle, but they do remain rare and expensive in spite of continuing attempts to cultivate them by planting oak seedlings inoculated with truffle spores. Some of these attempts have been encouraging and have resulted in good-sized harvests, but a truffle oak has a lifespan of only thirty years and takes at least seven years to produce its first truffles. All the same, nearly 90 percent of all truffle culture today comes from these truffle "farms" and with every prolonged dry spell the wild truffle of old loses more ground. Yet, it is unlikely that we will see mass-produced truffles anytime soon.

Less expensive, and available year-round, are the various derivatives, such as truffle oil, truffle paste, and even truffle juice obtained from squeezed truffles and used to flavor rice or sauces. I read somewhere that fashion designer Tom Ford came out with a perfume whose first ingredient is truffle scent. Better not wear this perfume to the farm if you don't want to risk pig encounters of a very close kind.

Christmas in Provence

November is gone and thoughts turn to Christmas. If in the United States the day after Thanksgiving marks the beginning of the Christmas season, in Provence the date is December 4th, the *Fête de la Sainte Barbe* (Barbara). On that day, people buy little packets of seeds of wheat which they sprinkle on wet cotton placed on saucers. By Christmas day, the wheat has grown tall and green and will serve as table decoration during Christmas dinner. This age-old custom served to ward off winter's rigors, accelerate the coming of spring and encourage the frozen earth to soon give way to a bountiful new harvest. During December, many shops and offices, including banks, have saucers with sprouting wheat on their counters and reception desks.

On the day of St. Barbara, Aix-en-Provence opens its *Marché des Santons*. The *Santons de Provence* are clay figurines, either plain or brightly painted, that are handcrafted by local artisans. Originally, these santons (little saints) were of biblical inspiration (nativity scene, shepherds, three Magi) but soon the creators began to include their fellow villagers in a variety of trades and professions, such as the miller with a sack of flour, the doctor with his instrument bag, the mayor in top hat and tricolor sash, the shoemaker, the butcher, the baker, the blacksmith. Other popular figurines are the beautiful Arlésiennes in traditional dress, peasants carrying produce or chickens to market, and women spinning wool at the wheel.

Though most santons still depict rural life in Provence, a santon maker created consternation some time ago when he introduced the likenesses of actor Gérard Depardieu and fashion designer Christian Lacroix (who hails from Arles) among his santons. The art of santon making dates from the nineteenth century and has been practiced by a few families for generations. Clearly, "novelties" were not appreciated and not welcome.

The typical Provençal *crèche* may include little houses, a windmill, a bakery shop, a bridge, the village café, the town hall with flag, perhaps a railroad station or a country inn, and provides the setting for the figurines of villagers and shepherds. People tend to buy at least a couple of new santons for their crèche every year and some local families boast large collections built up over several generations. Some churches draw crowds with their beautiful life-sized crèches of figures in Provençal dress gathered around the Nativity scene. Gifts of wheat, lavender, grapes or olives sometimes complement the Magi's myrrh and incense, and a sheep dog may join the ox and donkey.

The santons certainly add charm to the Provençal Christmas celebration, but when all is said and done Christmas in France is mostly about *food*. This is not a country for carolers, for office Christmas parties, for decking the halls or sending out numerous Christmas cards. Rather, all creativity seems focused on the table, and when you know that the average French family spends around $300 on Christmas dinner you can be sure that the results are impressive. *Se faire plaisir* is the order of the day, and half the pleasure is in the planning of the feast which starts long before the big day and doesn't end until the *digestif* has been passed around the table.

In our house, too, food is important and a lot of care is lavished on Christmas dinner, traditionally served on Christmas eve. Oscar scouts recipes for weeks before choosing the menu and wines, but the one constant is Christmas breakfast when each gets his wish: an American breakfast for Oscar (bacon, eggs, sausages, pancakes and maple syrup) and a truffle omelet for me if we are lucky enough to have truffles. After a long dry summer, truffles can be scarce and expensive (about €800–€1000 per kilo) and they usually don't reach full flavor until sometime in January.

But before this breakfast, we go to midnight mass at the Cathedral in Aix. The choir sings beautifully, the organ music is wonderful, but the best part for me is still the ringing of the church bells when mass is over.

A beautiful, deeply sonorous ringing of every single bell in the register over the quiet, sleeping, age-old city of Aix-en-Provence. It hits me in the gut every time. We go home to dessert and champagne, wish each other Merry Christmas and wake to a late breakfast and gifts the next morning. A perfect Christmas *à deux*.

A week before Christmas, a big tent is set up at the Rotonde in Aix for the next two weeks. This is where the new olive oil is introduced, where truffles are offered under the aegis of the Association of Truffle Growers (quality- and price-controlled), and where *Les Treize Desserts de Provence* are sold. The Thirteen Desserts are a local Christmas tradition that dates from times when people would have a light all-vegetable meal before midnight mass and then would have their dessert after church. The light meal is definitely a thing of the past, but the thirteen-part dessert (symbolizing Christ and his twelve apostles) survives. It consists of *Gibassié*, also called *Pompe à l'Huile* (a dry olive-oil and orange-zest cake to be dipped in sweet wine), black and white nougat, dried figs, raisins, nuts and almonds, white grapes, green winter melon, quince paste, dates, mandarins, and Calissons, the traditional sweets from Aix-en-Provence.

During the Christmas season food displays are often tantalizing. Or surprising, as in the case of our butcher who has a whole suckling pig in his window with a nosegay of fresh flowers sprouting from its rump. And the packages of fresh *foie gras* not only give the name and location of the farm that produced it but also a picture of the *gaveur*, the person who did the force-feeding. Meet the executioner! By the way, I learned that foie gras is not a French invention, since the old Romans and even the Egyptians were familiar with it. Birds would over-eat before taking off on long flights and when they were caught it was discovered that they were tastier than others, so the fatty liver became prized and the rest is history. Do you think this is a French fabulation to make you feel less guilty about eating force-fed fowl? Anyway, *si non è vero è ben trovato,* as the Romans say.

Although in this season food ads predominate in magazines, the large billboards seem to favor lingerie or perfume with superbly sexy ads. Women's bodies in every state of undress bid you hello and fare-thee-well from posters and photos. A particularly hot one is for Aubade, a lingerie brand, showing a back shot of a tight pair of *fesses* in the smallest hint of a bikini. Oscar still backpedals when he comes across one of those, unable to move on without one more lingering look at this Christmas treat. Another good one is a large poster of a young man leaning back on a couch with a serious, pensive look on his face, staring through two impossibly long spread legs standing in front of him on stiletto heels and ending in a pair of bare buttocks that may or may not be wearing a tanga slip—you know, the dental floss kind. The ad says: "Stop Thinking… ." I can't remember what they're selling but I sure remember the picture.

Time again for our annual year-end cocktail party, which has become a popular event. Oscar prepares an ample and varied buffet, but the Virginia honey-baked ham remains a favorite among our French friends. Last year many of them left with a very un-French doggy bag once they had overcome their initial resistance to this quaint American custom. Globalization at work?

Les Tripettes de Barjols

January is a month of many feasts in Provence. Truffles, olive oil, mimosa, saints—all are honored with a Fête. One of the most popular ones is the *Fête de St. Marcel*, also known as *Les Tripettes*, in Barjols, a little town in the Haut Var about an hour's drive from Aix-en-Provence. This is one of the oldest and most colorful celebrations in the area, going back to 1350 when the relics of Saint Marcel were brought to Barjols. Around the year 580, at age eighty, Saint Marcel went to Rome to report to the Pope on the state of his bishopric. On his return, exhausted from the long journey, he stopped off at a monastery in Montmeyan in the Haut Var, where he died and was buried. Soon, miracles began to occur that were attributed to the holy old man, he was proclaimed a saint, and his tomb became a site of pilgrimage.

In 1349, with the abbey in bad disrepair, St. Marcel appeared one night to the custodian and asked to have his remains moved to a more dignified spot. The towns of Barjols and Aups, equidistant from the dilapidated abbey, both laid claim to the holy remains—relics were a source of pilgrimage, the tourism of the day—and on the 17th of January 1350 a group of men from

Barjols, without further discussion, simply sneaked into the abbey church and removed the remains. On their way back to Barjols they encountered a group of women who were washing the tripes of a bull killed that day to commemorate the bull that years earlier had wandered into Barjols, then under siege, and saved the town from famine. The women dropped their tripes in a basket and followed the men with St. Marcel's relics to Barjols, where the joyous procession entered the collegiate church chanting "Saint Marcel, Saint Marcel, these tripes are for you!" Everyone in the church jumped and chanted and, voilà, the *Danse des Tripettes* was born. Ever since that day, the town of Barjols celebrates its patron saint St. Marcel on the weekend closest to the 17th of January.

For this weekend, every tree, shrub and potted plant in Barjols is decorated with red and yellow paper roses, the colors of Provence. The festivities start on Saturday morning with an aubade to the Authorities by the fife-and-drum groups and dancers in Provençal costume who perform a Farandole. Among the other participants are the *Gardians* of the Camargue on their white horses, various groups in period costume (heralds, knights in tights and tunics, ladies in brocaded long dresses and pointed veil-trailing hats), and the Bravades who later on will spend a lot of time shooting in the air.

And, of course, The Bull, a major player. He has been cleaned, brushed and decorated that morning before walking with his keeper to the main square to be admired by the Authorities and all those gathered there, who then march him to the church where he is blessed by the bishop, applauded by the people and finally led to the slaughterhouse for his offering. That mission accomplished, folklore breaks out all over town—the Gardians get to show their skills on horseback, the dancers dance, the fifers fife and a good time is had by all.

Sunday morning, a high mass in the old collegiate church shifts the focus to Saint Marcel, whose bust with relics takes center stage. The church is filled to bursting and the crowd spills outside, where I ended up finding a few square inches of space next to the portal. Not close enough to see inside but close enough to hear the service through loudspeakers mounted outside. At the end of mass, a joyous chant of "Saint Marcel, Saint Marcel...!" erupted from thousands of throats and a loud simultaneous rumble seemed to shake the old walls. This was the *Danse des Tripettes* which *everybody*, including the bishop, performed throughout the nine stanzas of the song. (The Tripettes consists of a jumping up and down in place, Masai-like).

Outside, the crowd joined in, young and old, mothers with babies, old ladies helped by younger ones, even the people in the windows surrounding the square—not a static one among them. *En masse* they jumped, singing and laughing as if fueled by magic mushrooms. Then the church began to empty—the faithful, the folkloric groups, the costumed nobles, and some menacing-looking men in chain mail and visors with blunderbusses.

When the first salvo rang within inches of my ear, spewing a cloud of smoke and bits of burning paper, I thought I saw my eardrums float by. Once I recovered,

I noticed how these blunderbussers put powder-packed four-inch-long paper cartridges in their barrel and packed them down with a long rod before shooting in the air. Unable to get away from them, I covered my ears and vowed to bring earplugs next time.

As the church continued to empty, the shooters and dancers and musicians formed a circle into which they welcomed, at last, the venerated bust of Saint Marcel, which was carried by a dozen beautifully costumed men and followed by the bishop and the parish priests. Once again, "Saint Marcel...!" was sung and the Tripettes danced, not only by the huge crowd but by the good saint and his bearers as well. For a moment I feared for the saint, whose bust is framed by an open gilded cage and topped by a white *plumeau*, like a feather duster. But when I saw the plumeau bobbing rhythmically above the crowd, I knew that all was well. The blunderbusses sounded a deafening finale and then the procession started moving through the narrow streets to the village green, where a huge spit had been erected for the roasting of the bull. After a tour of the green to the chanting of his name and the dancing of the Tripettes, Saint Marcel was then carried back to his church until next year.

Now the attention shifts to the bull who arrives *en broche* mounted high on a decorated wagon pulled by draught horses who slowly walk around the green, followed by the bands, the dancers and all the costumed parties, and deliver the bull to the giant spit in the center where the designated butcher and a dozen *marmitons*, his pint-sized little kitchen helpers, all clad in long white butcher's aprons, are waiting for him. There the bull is lowered from the wagon and suspended over a fire, to roast slowly for the remainder of the day. In the old days the meat was given to the poor, but nowadays it is sold the next day in one-pound portions. Once the bull starts roasting, the crowd disperses into cafés and restaurants to warm up and fill up, and to prepare for an afternoon of bonfires, music and dancing until dinner and the *Grand Bal* of the evening.

This historical Fête was briefly endangered in the 1980s when an animal-protection group protested the killing of a bull for these celebrations. Brigitte Bardot got into the fray and offered to buy the bull rather than have him killed. But the argument that the bull was killed in the slaughterhouse in the same manner as thousands of cattle in other slaughterhouses every day won out in the end, and today the *Fête de St. Marcel* continues to be celebrated as it has been since the fourteenth century.

Winter Festivities

In late January we celebrate the *Fête de St. Vincent* in Coudoux, a village about half an hour's drive from Aix-en-Provence. This is the annual homage to Saint Vincent, patron saint of the grape growers, who—legend has it—stopped one day with his donkey in a vineyard to chat with the field workers. When he returned to his donkey a few moments later, the animal had chewed a number of vine shoots. During the next harvest, these "eaten" plants turned out to be more heavily laden with grapes than the others. The donkey had introduced the pruning of the vines and Saint Vincent became the vintners' patron saint!

After the local priest has blessed the good saint's statue and thanked him for another bountiful harvest, the statue is carried around the village by folkloric groups, accompanied by a fife-and-drum band that plays the *Coupo Santo*, the national hymn of Provence. Once St. Vincent has been returned to his perch in the church, the festivities begin and the wine starts flowing. No homage without wine—not in Provence.

Another product they celebrate in Coudoux that day is olive oil, the wonderful thick green oil that is pressed by a small local mill through flat round coconut-fiber bags called *scourtins*—basically two woven disks sewn together except for an opening to insert the olive paste. Once the olives have been washed, they are ground, pits and all, by a big millstone and the resulting thick paste is scooped into the scourtins. These are then stacked twenty to thirty high on a hydraulic press and the oil slowly squeezed through the fibrous mats while the olive mush remains inside (this is a first cold pressing).

This age-old pressing method is in danger of disappearing because Brussels has decreed that all olive oil shall henceforth be produced in steel vats and in tiled, germ-free spaces. No more wooden presses and coco mats. The result will no doubt be more homogeneous but less fragrant, and many small producers will not be able to afford to "upgrade" their mills and will go out of business. It will be a loss, not only of one of life's small pleasures but also of the artisanal way of producing things. Of course, Oscar and I are supporting the old ways as much as we can—bitching about Brussels with the rest of them while drinking wine and eating bread dipped in olive oil—but I am afraid the technocrats will win in the end.

Say winter, say mimosa. Soon after Christmas, the first mimosa appears at our flower markets and a month later the town of Mandelieu-La Napoule, the mimosa capital near Cannes, celebrates with a two-week-long festival complete with a Mimosa Queen and large floats overflowing with the cheery yellow bloom, like so many rays of sunshine.

On the third Sunday of January, the town of Richerenches in the Vaucluse honors the truffle with a mass said in Provençal where one can give a truffle to the collection plate rather than money. The collected truffles are then sold at a public auction in front of the town hall, with the proceeds going to the church. And on two successive Sundays in February, the little port of Carry-le-Rouet, just outside Marseilles, celebrates the sea urchin (*oursin*) at its Oursinade, where stalls along the port offer the freshly caught spiky delicacy which is cut in half before your eyes so you can scoop out the tiny pink treasure it holds. Better than caviar, according to some.

By mid-February, get ready for Carnival in Nice or the lemon festival in nearby Menton. While many towns in different parts of France celebrate Carnival, Nice stands out for its extravagant parade, often under blue skies and always well attended by large crowds seeking a break from winter. No better place, however, for a winter break than Menton with its microclimate that practically guarantees you sun. There, within a stone's throw from Carnival-mad Nice, this climatically blessed enclave holds its lemon festival with impressive floats entirely made up of the citrus fruits for which it is famous. Watching those fragrant floats roll down the palm-tree-lined boulevards, it is indeed hard to believe that this is February and winter has another month to run.

Calissons, Navettes, and Brioches

Every year in early September we have the *Bénédiction des Calissons*, which celebrates the deliverance of Aix-en-Provence from the plague. Aix, like many other parts of Europe, had repeatedly been ravaged by the plague when, in 1629, it was hit again. In an attempt to protect the citizenry, the city fathers sequestered the people to their houses and constructed on each street corner, above the ground floor, a niche with a statue of the Virgin Mary to which they could pray from their windows. (Many of these oratories survive to this day, as well as some of the large advertisements that clever merchants managed to paint on nearby walls).

When this did not slow down the plague the local notables decided to leave the city, but not before a desperate last appeal was made to the Virgin of the Seds, patron saint of Aix-en-Provence, at a high mass during which a local almond-paste sweet was used instead of bread which was not available. This soft candy being handed out from the chalice (*la calice*) came to be known as the Calisson.

The Virgin heard, the plague passed, and ever since then the City of Aix-en-Provence has been giving thanks on the first Sunday of September. The ceremony, which takes place inside and in front of the Church of St. John of Malta, is very colorful, with singers and dancers in traditional Provençal costume, the brotherhood of *Les Patissiers de Calissons* in whites with toque, fife-and-drum bands, and—surprise—Louis XIV with his mother Anne of Austria, in wig and full regalia, accompanied by half a dozen children dressed in brocades and finery of the time. It made for a very pretty picture, although Louis XIV was not even born at the time of the event that was being celebrated.

Then everybody moved inside the church, where a choir sang, the archbishop spoke some appropriate words and blessed the calissons that were displayed in baskets on the altar, and the costumed children sat prettily on the altar steps. One tired little boy among them, perhaps three years old, decided to lie down. As the last notes died down and people filed out behind the blessed calissons that were going to be handed out on the church square, the last priest to leave the altar noticed a little lump, all brocade and lace, on the altar steps. The little page boy was so sound asleep that he had to be carried outside. I hope somebody saved a calisson for him.

In early February another sweet is celebrated, this time in Marseilles where the traditional *Navette* was born. The origin of this boat-shaped biscuit is claimed by both the Roman Catholic Church and by local superstition. Again, the church takes the lead as the archbishop celebrates *La Chandeleur* (Candlemas, when Jesus was presented in the Temple), and recalls the very first such celebration by the Phoceans, Greek sailors who founded Marseilles more than twenty-six hundred years ago when they arrived by boat and established Massalia. To some, the boat-shaped cookie is meant to replicate this ancestral Phocean vessel, while for the archbishop it represents the arrival of Christ's word and Christianity on the Mediterranean shores.

Before the celebratory mass at Saint Victor's in the old port of Marseilles, cadets of the Merchant Marine academy sail out to Pointe Rouge, some ten kilometers down the coast, and carry back the Gospel as well as the statue of the Black Virgin who guards St. Victor's crypts that hold the remains of the martyrs. Baskets of *Navettes* spread their delicate orange scent throughout the church before they get blessed by the archbishop and handed out after mass.

If you miss these church-blessed freebies, rest assured that any self-respecting *patisserie* in this area will be glad to sell you the paying kind.

Finally, the village of Maillane celebrates its patron saint Agatha on February 5th with *brioches* baked in the form of a female breast, commemorating the martyrdom of Agatha whose breasts were cut off. In Provence, Christianity and paganism still find their way into food.

Salon de l'Agriculture
or Chirac's Farewell to Farms

All right, we are no longer in Provence, Toto, but to stay in the spirit of food for the moment I invite you to come with me to Paris, to the mother of all food fairs. It is worth leaving Provence for—at least for a day.

So this is Paris in March 2007, and the forty-fourth annual *Salon de l'Agriculture* has just closed its doors at the Porte de Versailles, where some six hundred thousand visitors enjoyed this "largest farm of France" and all that comes with it: more than three acres of exhibits with every breed of cattle, sheep, goats, pigs, fish and fowl. In other words, anything that walks, swims, waddles or flies and ends up on the French dinner table. Not to mention nine breeds of draught horses, and various mules and donkeys, all brushed and polished to a high gloss. Literally—I saw a farmer dust and spit-polish the horns of a prized cow, ending with a snap of the cloth just like the best of shoe shiners.

This gigantic Salon, spread over several buildings, has six hundred and fifty exhibitors from all regions of France, including one hundred seventy-nine wineries, and fifty restaurants that cater to every purse and every taste. It's the farm in the city—a showplace for the biggest and the best in farm animals, a petting zoo, a forum for fish farming and aquaculture, for equestrian tourism, for organic farming, for wind and solar energy, horticulture, food processing and on and on. The French are deeply attached to their *terroir* and will defend tooth and nail the farming methods of their fathers and grandfathers, and of course the indefensible subsidies that allow these methods to continue. And they will be only too happy to sample the products of these methods—the ham, the lamb, the beef, the cheese, the charcuterie, the *foie gras*—the entire "made in France" gamut of food that is presented at the Salon and offered freely at every turn. The best in the world, all seem to agree. They may have a point but, frankly, when it comes to beef yours truly thinks the Argentines and the Americans have it. Hands down.

For ten days in March, the Salon is *the* ticket in Paris. In attendance, it easily outperforms Fashion Week and the Rolland Garros tennis tournament, perhaps because this is a family affair. Lots of children here, who love to stroke and pet the merchandise before they follow their parents in tasting every tidbit offered. They may wash theirs down with milk or organic apple juice while their parents reach for the wine, but all seem to fill up happily. Farms are about food, after all, so no one is shy. For entertainment, there's nothing like animals to delight the crowd. Here's the truffle dog digging up truffles, the sheepdog rounding up sheep, and a dozen piglets pushing and pulling the life out of a huge sow. While children are drawn to the smaller animals, adults seem mesmerized by the powerful bulls whose enormous strength seems barely restrained by the heavy iron chain that bolts them to the wall.

The *Salon de l'Agriculture* draws large crowds and a huge television audience, and, inevitably, a swarm of politicians. This being a presidential election year, the place was dense with politicians fighting for face time on national television. Cushioned by their entourage and careful to avoid each other, they were all eager to taste and toast in front of cameras and make the usual promises. "If I am elected," said contender Nicolas Sarkozy, "I will allow advertising for wines again in France." Socialist Ségolène Royal came and went without impressing the farmers, who are traditionally to the right.

And then there was First Farmer Jacques Chirac, who delared: "France will stand firm against British Peter Mandelson (European Commissioner of Commerce) who favors the United States in his negotiations with the World Trade Commission." It is no secret that French farmers roundly detest "Brussels" where their future is decided by bureaucrats, nor is it a secret that Jacques Chirac, who was Minister of Agriculture under Georges Pompidou, is the farmers' friend and defender.

He has been coming to the *Salon de l'Agriculture* for thirty-five years now, and is always warmly received. Never in a hurry, he spent nearly five hours at the Salon this year, the last one in his political life. He eats and drinks everything that is offered to him, and seems to genuinely enjoy himself. "How much does she weigh?" he asks about a big cow. "Bravo!" and an affectionate pat on a huge behind before he moves on to the next stall and the next question or comment. He knows how to talk about cattle and pigs and fowl, and has been heard to discuss recipes along the way. Unlike his rather stiff appearance at formal occasions and his poor rating as a public speaker, among the farm crowd Chirac seems totally at ease. He happily stops for photographs and does not hesitate to kiss a piglet or take one in his arms. Sure, he kisses babies too but gives the impression that he is more comfortable with animals.

Before leaving, he was heard to congratulate the organizers of this "superb Salon that does great honor to French agriculture and to France." Not bad for his farewell to farms, and he may even mean it. But even if he didn't, he will be missed here. Many are those who see Chirac's agricultural policies as protectionist and damaging to emerging countries that can supply France with corn or other crops at a fraction of the subsidized price in France, but you won't see them here at the Salon. For thirty-five years Chirac has obstinately defended the French family farm and its traditional ways, and the farmers know there is no one in the current presidential line-up who can fill his shoes. In the complex world of globalization and the newly extended Europe of twenty-seven member-nations, the survival of the French family farm is by no means a sure thing.

Camargue

One of the most interesting and untouched regions of southern France is the Camargue, a 360-square-mile area located in the delta formed by the two arms of the river Rhône before they spill into the Mediterranean. In 1927, nearly two-thirds of the total surface of the Camargue was set aside as a nature reserve and it was granted National Park status in 1970. The remaining one-third consists of agricultural land in the north that produces cereals, rice and grapes, and salt flats in the south where the Romans already collected salt in their day, followed in the Middle Ages by Cistercian and Benedictine monks who began to exploit the salt pans for commercial purposes.

The protected Camargue National Park, which attracts more than a million tourists every year, is mostly marshland and contains several large brine lagoons where thousands of pink flamingos from Africa come to nest every spring, feeding on the tiny shrimp that give them their pink color. With more than 400 species of birds the reserve is a birdwatcher's paradise, but it is also known for the white horses and black bulls that live here in semi-liberty. The Camargue horse is native to the area and it is thought that this historic breed is the one depicted in the Paleolithic cave paintings of Lascaux in the southwest. Today, its broad hooves are an evolutionary adaptation to the wet marshland, and the present-day Camargue horse is never shod. This "white" horse is actually born black or brown and does not fade to white until its fourth year.

The black bull raised in the Camargue is a bit smaller than the Spanish Miura fighting bull, and is mostly used in the popular *Course Camarguaise* in village arenas where bulls are not killed, although some of the bigger and more aggressive ones may be sent to Arles or Nîmes for the regular bullfights. The cattle ranches where these bulls are bred are called *manades* and the cowboys who manage these bulls are the *Gardians* that you see at every village festival. They themselves are a tough breed, living year-round in the extreme climate of the Camargue (hot, humid and mosquito-infested summers, cold and wind-battered winters) where they are housed in little thatch-roofed, often windowless houses that protect them from the fierce elements, with bulls' horns over the door to ward off evil spirits.

The "capital" of the Camargue is Arles at the northernmost tip, where the Rhône splits into two branches to form the largest river delta in western Europe. Arles in the north with its Roman arenas, and Aigues Mortes in the south, where Saint Louis (Louis IX) established a port in the 13th century as a staging point for his crusades, have plenty to offer the history buff. The recent discovery of a life-size sculpted bust of Caesar in the Rhône near Arles—his only extant "portrait" complete with wrinkles and hollowed cheeks, tentatively dated 46 BC—adds to the richness of Roman artifacts in the area and underscores the importance of Arles in the Roman empire of southern France.

But not all local history is as grandiose or as ancient, as I found out when I discovered an American connection. It appears that in 1905 Buffalo Bill and his Wild West Congress of Rough Riders of the World visited the area and put on a number of shows, including one in Marseilles. They were the guests of Folco de Baroncelli who had seen them earlier in Nîmes and invited them to his cattle ranch near Saintes-Maries-de-la-Mer where, always fascinated by Indians, he was eager to meet in person the Sioux from Dakota that traveled with wild Bill Cody, a.k.a. Buffalo Bill. This visit was the beginning of a lasting friendship between one of the Sioux, Jacob White Eyes, and his host. They were never to meet again, but corresponded for years and developed such a strong bond that White Eyes bestowed the Indian name "True Bird" on his soul brother from the Camargue.

A year later Baroncelli met Joe Hamman, a French moviemaker and fellow aficionado of American-Indian culture, who subsequently shot a number of "American westerns" in the Camargue, assisted by Baroncelli who recruited the local extras and rounded up the horses and bulls used in these productions. From their extensive reading, both men were familiar enough with the American West and the Indian culture to give these made-in-Camargue "westerns" an authentic cowboy-and-Indian look.

If the Camargue has a local hero and benefactor it is the eccentric Marquis Folco de Baroncelli (1869–1943) whose noble Italian ancestors came from Florence but subsequently moved to France where Folco was born in Aix-en-Provence in 1869. With the prestige of his noble title and his family money, Baroncelli was destined to have a comfortable life of bourgeois respectability, but he fell in love with the Camargue and with its poor and sparse local population, and decided to dedicate his life to the preservation of this untouched wilderness and to the betterment of local living conditions. It is largely thanks to his efforts that the Camargue was declared a nature reserve and that the *Nacioun Gardiano*, dedicated to the preservation of the language and traditions of the Camargue, flourishes today. Baroncelli spoke Provençal, lived for more than 40 years in the harsh climate of the Camargue, and spent his fortune fighting for its protection. He died broke in 1943 at age 74, shortly after the Germans requisitioned his ranch.

If Baroncelli were alive today, he might have mixed feelings about the ecotourism that is driving the economic survival of the Camargue National

Park, where roads have been created (although few paved ones) and bed-and-breakfasts and restaurants now cater to the visitors. Hiking, bicycling and bird watching allow people to enjoy nature and the rich biodiversity up close, and for the hardier souls the spirited Camargue horses can be rented for guided or unguided rides through the marshes and on the empty beaches of this unspoilt wilderness. It is a delicate dance to maintain the fragile balance between indigenous ecosystems and human activities, but even Baroncelli knew that his beloved Camargue can only survive with the help of visitors who, we may hope, will share his love for this unique place and pay it the respect it deserves.

Spring

Normally, spring should have sprung in abundance by mid-May but this year spring has come and gone numerous times already, each time making way for cold, windy weather and even snow. Last weekend, there was new snowfall in the Alps and a road in the Jura was closed by an avalanche. Every time we have two sunny days in a row we throw open all the windows, turn our faces to the sun and sigh "at last!"—only to be disappointed again. Yet, some signs point unequivocally to spring, such as our herb garden (a flower box in the kitchen window).

After a recent trip to Paris, we came home to find that a pigeon had laid two eggs next to the rosemary. Ma pigeon got awfully nervous when I tried to water the rosemary, so we are holding off on our planting of basil and thyme. Meanwhile the eggs have hatched and two shivering little lumps of dirty-yellow fuzz have appeared. They are blind and scrawny, with pink beaks that are beginning to turn grey, and look pathetically ugly. To their mother, however, they must be pure perfection and she and Pa pigeon alternate sitting protectively on their pitiful progeny.

Feeding sessions are quite a sight: regurgitated food that scrawn gets deep from his mother's throat, stretching high and trembling with excitement and want. During this process mother seems to inflate herself and make brisk little movements, probably to position the food just so. When she catches me watching her she stops everything and stares at me from her sideways position, fixing me with one accusing unblinking eye until I withdraw in embarrassment. I am quite fascinated by the whole process and can't wait to see the monotonous menu change from regurgitata to worms and perhaps insects. Or are pigeons too lumpy to catch insects on the fly? I am very ignorant about these things and am learning as I go. Different from Art History or The Kings of France or some such retirement course I had in mind, but very satisfying just the same.

My new-found fascination with the wonders of nature was rudely interrupted, however, when I found my wee pigeons dying one afternoon. They were killed by a predator not half an hour after I had last seen them happily snuggled together, getting nice and round and beginning to lose their down. I think that in another two or three weeks they might have been far enough along to leave the nest. It was horrible to find them all bloodied and mangled, in broad daylight, apparently by another bird. Our planter box is in a deeply recessed window on the front of the house three floors up and completely out of reach of cats. It looked like some hate crime, slashed and pecked as they were by a sharp beak. Shortly after I removed them, the mother pigeon came up to the window, craning her neck as if to see into the far corners of the kitchen, then flew off to the rooftop across the street from where she kept staring into the empty nest. With their silly expressionless bird faces you wonder what they think, but seeing her there on the roof you could tell this was an unhappy pigeon.

I do miss those baby birds, having followed them from egg to well-fed little lump, all along marveling at nature's ways. Well, I got a look at nature's cruel side and did not care for it. The next day, in a catering shop in town I saw some plump little birds about the size of my little pigeons wrapped in a slice of bacon, and I realized that birds get killed commercially every day for people like us. Just the same, I don't think I will be ordering quail anytime soon.

———•———

Another sign of spring is the sudden proliferation of advertisements for weight-losing schemes and skin-firming products, as always promoted by beautiful bodies and glowing skin. "Get ready for the beach!" they urge from billboards and magazine pages and pharmacy counters. Curiously, France has more pharmacies than I ever saw in any other country. They all carry toiletries and beauty products as well, including those of the ever-expanding "anti-aging" variety. Anti-aging toothpaste, shampoo, hair cream—surely, we'll have anti-aging nail polish soon. The French love to pamper their bodies and care a great deal about their appearance, but they seem equally fond of pills and potions and are among the biggest antibiotics users in the world—perhaps aided by a very generous *Sécurité Sociale* (the national health system). When I first signed up for the lovely Roman thermal baths in Aix a couple of years ago, I was surprised to be told that this was no longer covered by the *Sécurité Sociale*. Before then, it seems, a popular prescription for stress was a "cure" at a health spa, but today doctors go the less expensive Prozac route.

In May there are three official holidays: *la Fête du Travail* (May 1st), Ascension, and Pentecost, and so far we have had four strikes. Not the most productive month. Our strikers have been railroad workers, postal workers, cauliflower growers (yes, they blocked roads, made a lot of noise and just got damages from the government to make up for tumbling prices), and the service workers of the Hotel Carlton in Cannes where lots of stars are staying for the Film Festival that takes place there in May and draws worldwide attention. Welcome to France! Perhaps the memory of "Mai '68"—the Paris student riots and general strike that brought down the government of Charles de Gaulle—makes the French frisky in the month of May.

Around this time, the familiar click of *Boules* fills the air in every village and makes us dust off our own set of balls. We are getting Frencher every day. It's fun and, what's more, it's our speed. We usually play boules with friends at their houses, fueled by rosé wine, and bending the rules when it suits us. In spite of occasional cheating, these matches are great fun, especially since they are usually followed by dinner outdoors. Come to think of it, everything seems followed by dinner here.

Easter in Provence
Tienta and Feria

Easter is *Feria* time down here, with bullfights in the Roman arenas of Arles and Nîmes. These are the traditional corridas where bulls are killed, with picadors on horseback, matadors in their *traje de luz* and all the ancient rituals. For four days in a row, these corridas draw the usual aficionados and tourists, and fill the streets with enormous copper pans of paella and trumpet music and paso-doble dancers.

It's a world removed from the *Tienta*, a less well-known event which takes place on Easter-Monday morning in the village of Fontvieille. A *tienta* is a test of young cows that are selected to be bred with fighting bulls. They are challenged with the cape and the muleta to test their agility and their fighting spirit, but no blood is spilled.

Here, the public is not exactly the Hemingway crowd. Rather, these people come armed with baguettes, sausages, pâté, cheese and lots of wine, to be entertained while they eat. Bread and circus, as of old. An occasional muffled "Olé" escapes a sausage-stuffed mouth, but nobody gets too excited. The breeders are the only attentive ones, and they may even take their cow through a Veronica themselves. It's fun in the sun, even for the animals.

For most of them, that is, because the very first cow we saw died of a heart attack. She had all the right moves and the required fighting spirit, but she didn't know when to stop. Apparently, young animals sometimes get so excited that they blow their fuses, so to speak. When this cow went through her knees and would not get up, they threw a bucket of cold water in her face—just like in the boxing ring. Then the "experts" gathered around and soon someone was doing a heart massage, but to no avail. The pick-up truck hauled her out of the arena, to applause, and the breeder took a loss. On to the next cow, until twenty of them had been tested.

The "bullfighters" were a varied lot, including one boy who seemed no more than twelve years old. He was being coached by his father from the sidelines with shouts of *Au museau!* (to the muzzle!) and *Ne recule pas!* (don't step back!). [Right, dad, why don't *you* come over here?] But the kid did just fine, as did everyone else that day. After the last cow, the mayor invited all those present to come down and have a drink in the arena to celebrate the twenty-fifth anniversary of the local Tienta, and we were offered pastis, vermouth and whiskey! The whiskey may have been in honor of Peter Mayle who has brought hordes of Brits and others to Provence. Anyway, it was an unusual touch.

From cows to bulls is but a small step, and this being Easter Monday we decided to take the short drive to Arles and see if we were ready for the real thing. After all these years of trying to do as the locals do, we felt it was time to take the bullfight plunge. Tauromachy is alive and well in Provence and of all the places where corridas are still being performed Arles is the undisputed leader, where some of the big names from Spain come to fight before a well-informed public. There are two bullfights a day for four days and Arles goes completely mad, with non-stop music in the streets, food stalls (paella), bodegas for wine, beer and pastis everywhere, and special photo-filled daily newspapers. The party goes on until dawn every day and doesn't stop until Tuesday morning when, somehow, most people get back to work.

As for the corrida we saw—all right, I'll say it—it was beautiful. To see the ritualistic pageantry of the magnificently dressed toreador and his entourage of banderilleros, picadors on horseback and assistants carrying capes, advancing slowly toward the President's box in the huge Roman arena that fairly oozes *Christians and Lions*, is to be awed by the sheer beauty and solemnity of the moment. And once the trumpet music stills, the helpers withdraw behind barricades and the toreador finds himself alone in the middle of the arena, in total silence, ready to face a ferocious animal with no more than a piece of cloth, you tense in your seat and scream "*Olé!*" when he swirls the bull around him without giving an inch. If you saw Almodovar's movie "Talk to Her" you know what a mad bull looks like up close and you shudder. Luckily, our corrida was a good one with two of the three bullfighters getting two ears each, but not without a tremendous ruckus and a sea of white handkerchiefs and thumb-downs from the stands when the public disagreed with the presiding judge awarding only one ear when two were considered appropriate. This was a *Roman* arena, after all.

Cézanne and John Rewald

Aix-en-Provence has a famous native son: Paul Cézanne (1839–1906). In fact, it has two famous sons: Cézanne and Emile Zola (1840–1902). They met in high school where they discovered in each other a kindred spirit drawn to the arts—Cézanne to painting and Zola to writing. Their close friendship was to last for many years, until Zola published "l'Oeuvre" in 1886, a novel about a doomed artist which Cézanne considered to be an unflattering portrait of himself. Cézanne never forgave Zola and the two parted ways.

Each achieved fame in his field; Zola rather quickly, Cézanne only after years of struggle.

Cézanne's father, who was a hat manufacturer and later a banker in Aix-en-Provence, wanted his son to join the ranks of the bourgeoisie he had himself recently penetrated and insisted that Paul become a lawyer. Against his natural inclination to paint and to go to art school, Paul obeyed his father and finished law school. He worked briefly for his father's bank but showed no aptitude for business and was finally allowed to go to art school in Paris, where he met Pissaro, Renoir, and Degas. He learned to paint in the style of his day, copied masterworks in the Louvre and began submitting paintings to the *Salon*, where year after year his work would be refused. He never had a picture accepted by the *Salon* and finally, with a few artist friends, broke away from the main movements and joined the *Salon des Refusés* where the rejected works could be shown.

He returned from Paris to settle in Provence, bringing his model Hortense Fiquet with him who three years later bore him a son. Cézanne hid this relationship from his father who was still supporting him, and it was not until seventeen years later—just months before his father's death—that Paul Cézanne married his mistress and Cézanne *père* discovered that he had a grandson. A generous inheritance finally allowed Cézanne to provide comfort to his wife and son, and some time later to buy a plot of land on the hilly outskirts of Aix-en-Provence where he built a studio.

During his years in Aix, Cézanne had the bad luck to have a falling out with the director of the local museum who blocked his path at every turn and will forever be remembered for having declared: "As long as I am the director here there will never be a painting of yours in this museum." To this day, the Musée Granet does not own a single major work by its world-famous citizen.

Fortunately, the rest of the art world saw things differently, notably some American collectors such as Dr. Albert Barnes (Barnes Foundation in Merion, PA) and museums in Philadelphia, Washington DC, New York City, Chicago, the Hermitage Palace in Saint Petersburg, and many others.

Over the years Cézanne developed an obsession with the Montagne Sainte Victoire, a 3000-foot table-shaped mountain just outside Aix, which he painted close to 100 times from various observation points and in different lights. [An aside: When Picasso, who admired Cézanne, left his Riviera residence for the village of Vauvenargues near Aix to be closer to his beloved bullfights in the Roman arenas of Arles and Nîmes, he bought the Chateau de Vauvenargues located at the foot of the Montagne Sainte Victoire. In an enthusiastic note to Louis Kahnweiler, his Paris dealer, he wrote: "I bought Cézanne's Montagne Sainte Victoire" and when Kahnweiler asked "Which one?" Picasso answered "The real one!". Indeed, the chateau came with a good number of acres on the north face of the mountain. Today, both Picasso and his widow Jacqueline are buried on the grounds of the Chateau in the shadow of the Montagne Sainte Victoire.]

From his newly built studio, which lay within walking distance from some of his favorite sites, Cézanne would set out in the morning and spend all day painting outdoors, until one day in the fall of 1906 a sudden rain shower soaked him, he caught pneumonia and died days later. The studio was locked up and abandoned. That would have been the end of the *Atelier Cézanne* if John Rewald, noted Cézanne scholar, had not stepped in to save it for posterity.

John Gustave Rewald (1912–1994) was a German-born American art historian and recognized authority on Impressionism and Post-Impressionism. After studies at several German universities he moved to France in 1939 where he wrote his dissertation at the Sorbonne on the friendship between Cézanne and Zola. Because of his Jewish background he emigrated to the United States in 1941. There, he consulted for the NY Museum of Modern Art, organized exhibitions for it and other museums and wrote *The History of Impressionism*, which was published in 1946 to universal acclaim. Other books followed, among them *The History of Post-Impressionism*, which were widely admired not only for their solid scholarship but also for the quality of their prose. He was a visiting professor at Princeton, joined the faculty of the University of Chicago, and in 1974 was appointed as "distinguished professor of art history" at the City University of New York (CUNY). In 1977 he organized a major exhibition at MOMA: "Cézanne: The Late Work."

Helped by his eminent standing in the international art world, Rewald was instrumental in creating a foundation to save Cézanne's studio and turn it into a museum. Today, the *Atelier Cézanne* looks just like it did when Cézanne walked out of it that fatal day in October 1906, and it has become one of the most popular tourist stops in Aix-en-Provence. The city of Aix rewarded Rewald by naming a street after him.

Although Rewald died in New York City he is buried at Saint Pierre cemetery in Aix-en-Provence, across the path from Cézanne. It seems appropriate that he joined in death the man he had spent so much of his life studying and bringing to the attention of the world—in the place that Cézanne himself never managed to extricate himself from.

Lost in Translation

One of the pleasures of living in France is the language and the numerous bookstores. It is a bit of a surprise, therefore, to discover how little respect the French have for languages other than their own. On French radio and television Anglo-Saxon names are regularly tortured beyond recognition, and every foreign word—no matter what its origin—comes out sounding French. All English-language television programs are dubbed, with famous drawlers like John Wayne and Clint Eastwood speaking in staccato French. The French love American movies as long as they are in French.

Yet, France is still the first tourist destination in the world and in cities like Paris and Aix-en-Provence a timid effort is being made to accommodate non-French-speaking visitors. This can have surprising results, sometimes missing their intended goal but all the richer for it.

To see what I mean, take a look at the menu of the restaurant at the TGV train station in Aix-en-Provence. Let your eye wander over the long list of *plats* which are proposed in French and translated for our Anglo-Saxon visitors. Those visitors soon realize that what looks like English at first sight is… eh… well, eh… It's funny, is what it is. Judge for yourself.

Jambon Cru (which you all know as Raw Ham) is helpfully rendered as "Believed Ham" for our English-speaking friends.

Croque-Monsieur = Crunch Mister

Canapés à la Crevette = Shrimp Sofas

Herbes de Provence = Grasses of Provence

Salade à l'Huile d'Olive = Salad to the Olive Oil

Andouillette (a rather strong-flavored sausage) remains untranslated but…
Andouillette Arrosée de son Jus de Moutarde à l'Ancienne
        becomes
Sprinkled Andouillette of its Mustard Juice to Old

Brochettes de Volaille Grillée servies avec une sauce barbecue
        becomes
Roasted Poultry Skewers been useful with a sauce barbecue

The *Assiette Américaine* which is your familiar "Hamburger on a sesame bun"
        becomes

ROUND LOAF WITH SESAME SEEDS FURNISHED WITH
    A CHOPPED STEAK

Moving right along to *Nos Poissons* ("Our Fishes"),
    we find that

Dos de Colin Meunière
    becomes
HAKE MILLER BACK

Pavé de Saumon Nappé de Sauce Toscane
    turns into
NAPPÉ TUSCAN SAUCE SALMON PAVING STONE
I admit that the paving stone I had was very tasty.

Perhaps the best category of all is the Desserts:

Nos Douceurs, translated as OUR SOFTNESSES (!)

Here we find an English translation for brownies
    (little did you know you needed one).

Brownies au Chocolat
    becomes
BROWNIES WITH THE CHOCOLATE
    explained as:
    (*Un biscuit chocolat aux noix nappé de sauce au
    chocolat chaud, et bordé de crème montée)*
        or
    (A biscuit chocolate with nuts nappé of sauce to the
    chocolate hot and bordered of assembled cream)

Tarte Tatin = TATIN TART
> (*Pate feuilletée au beurre recouverte de quartiers de pommes fraiches poêlées au beurre et caramelisées, servie avec chantilly*)
>> or
> (Puff pastry with butter covered with districts of fresh to butter and caramelized apples, served with chantilly)

Coupe Delice = DELIGHT COUPE
> (*3 boules chocolat, vanille, rhum raisin, Chantilly avec son biscuit*)
>> or
> (3 balls chocolate, vanilla, rum grape, chantilly with its biscuit)

Once we stopped laughing we ordered one Fish and one Softness each, and enjoyed:

- 1 Hake Miller Back
- 1 Tatin Tart with extra districts of apples
  and
- 1 Salmon Paving Stone
- 1 Brownie nappé to the chocolate hot, but not bordered with assembled cream

The computer had not translated the wine list, for which I was rather grateful.

Franglais

Aaahh, the joys of Franglais! I just came across yet another version of the peculiar French use of the word "people." In France, it is an adjective that means something akin to our "socially prominent." A person described as "très people" (pr. peepull, rhymes with dull) would be a socialite to you and me. But "people" can also apply to a place, for instance, "St. Tropez est très people," as Beverly Hills would no doubt be. In the recent French presidential campaign, candidates were looking for "du soutien people" which is not the support of the people but of famous people, i.e., stars. For example, Johnny Halliday, the French Elvis Presley, came out in support of Nicolas Sarkozy on the right, while Ségolène Royal, the candidate on the left, obtained the backing of Catherine Deneuve. Signing up "un people" is part of a winning strategy, which led the serious French newspaper *Le Monde* to talk about "la pipolisation" of political campaigns.

Similarly, "la presse people" has nothing to do with people from the press but refers to gossipy or entertainment magazines and tabloids with lots of pictures, such as our *People* magazine. Whatever meaning is ascribed to "people" (or "pipole" as it is also spelled), it always is used in the singular, even in the term "boat people" for those refugees who fled by boat. One such person was described in the French press as "un boat people" who made good in France. There may have been a thousand people on the boat, but to the French each and every one of them is "un boat people."

The singular/plural business is a complicated one in France. Not in French, of course, just in "English." Thus, the French speak not only of "un people" when they mean one person but also of "un Marines" when they mean one Marine (as in Iraq). And then there are "un jean" or "un short" or "un comics" (comic strip), as well as a new skin cream that promises to give "du peps" to your face.

The French have a love affair with English names and expressions, even if there exist perfectly adequate equivalents in French. French business terms have given way to English, and not only in the world of technology. Thus, the perfectly clear French "Gérant" has become Manager (pr. manageur) or the unfortunate "Manageuse." "Un Must" has entered the French dictionary, as have the verbs "coacher" and "benchmarker," while "Le Making Of" is part of every French DVD. We have a flower shop called "Flowers Powers" as well as a hair salon called "Clean" and another one called "Wax" (where they do no waxing), for no other reason than that these English names are attractive to the owners.

Among French television programs, we have: "Le Bestophe" (Best of...) by the network that brought you

"Bigdil" (Big Deal). People sometimes ask you for a "postite" (pr. posteet) which is a yellow Post-It sticker. They clean their paint brushes with "du white" which is short for White Spirit (turpentine), they surf "le ouèbe" on their computers and send you "un mèl" unless their computer has a "bogue."

The hard-rock kind of fashion with torn jeans, safety pins, tattoos and extreme hair is called "destroy," as in "cette fille est très destroy." "Un sweat" (pr. sweet) would be a workout suit and "baskets" (pr. basKETS) are sneakers. For the sports minded there is also "le hand" and "le foot" for handball and football, and a tennis player is called a "tennisman." No known term for a female player, but in the last winter Olympics a French "snowbordeuse" won gold.

After a bit of "footing" (jogging) and a drop-off at "le pressing" (drycleaners), you could stop at the hairdresser's for a "brushing" (blow-dry), before you go to your "scrapbooking" club where your fellow "scrapbookeuses" are expecting you.

In a strange twist, our walkie-talkie becomes a "talkie-walkie" in French, and our pretzel becomes a "bretzel."

Here, "raveurs" go to rave parties where they meet "taggeurs" who paint graffiti ("tags" are graffiti). "Un break" is a stationwagon and "fioul" is what you burn to heat your house. But a "douche" in French is a shower in America, whereas an American douche is not a French shower. It can all get very tricky…

Franglais is alive and well in the food department also, as in this restaurant in Arles that claims to specialize in International Fooding. And gastronomy was given a boost at the "Semaine du Fooding" in Paris, where you were invited to "manger avec feeling" what some great chefs had prepared. The idea was to give people a taste without giving them a lesson, said Alexandre Cammas, its president. For further details, he referred to their website www.lefooding.com. The new cover of a fancy restaurant's menu now reads "Drinking and Fooding." And you knew of course that the Parisian restaurant *Le Train Bleu* features Grumble Cake for dessert.

Being cool in France is not what you think it is. "*Je serai plus cool la semaine prochaine*" would mean "I will have more time next week." This week, for instance, you might be "*stressé*," but next week your agenda is open.

Summer magazines always have Get-In-Shape advice, including firming-up exercises before hitting the beach. I read about a "*baby boomeuse*" who just followed instructions and ended up with a "*corps body buildé*" in pre-pregnancy shape. Getting in shape is another way of saying "relooker," which you can do with your face, your hair style or your dining room.

Sometimes we are invited to "un coquetelle" where we'll do our best to understand the English terms for some of the goodies served as we accept a bite of "crombole" (crumb cake) and join a discussion about the latest trends in "fooding" while the "eefee" (hi-fi) plays softly in the background.

Now that we're into pronunciation, what sounds like "Are DeesCOONT" turns out to be a hard (deep) discount. And when French radio announcers talk of:

Teemo CeleRIE
AldOOS UxLAY
Deek SheNAY
KeesharETTE, and
TreVORE PeeNOCK,

it takes a minute to realize they mean:

Timothy Leary
Aldous Huxley
Dick Cheney
Keith Jarrett, and
Trevor Pinnock

I am rather pleased with myself when I finally get it.

Gypsy Pilgrimage

A giant wave of caravans hits the beach town of Saintes-Maries-de-la-Mer in the Camargue every spring, when an estimated ten thousand gypsies from all over Europe gather there to celebrate their patron saint Black Sara on May 24th and 25th. Many of these *Gens du Voyage* (the politically correct term that replaced *gitans* or *tsiganes*) arrive a week in advance, so that babies born during the past year may be baptized by "their" local chaplain and newly formed couples may be married. But first and foremost, the gypsies are there to celebrate their black madonna Sara.

According to legend, Marie-Salomé and Marie-Jacobé, who were close to Jesus, fled the persecutions in their native Judea in a little boat, accompanied by their servant Sara, Lazarus, Martha, Mary Magdalene, and Maximin. Divine winds blew their boat ashore at what is today Saintes-Maries-de-la-Mer in southern France. While the others departed in various directions, the two Maries and Sara settled down and began to evangelize the locals as well as some roaming gypsies. Those gypsies felt a special affinity for Sara who was born in Egypt and had dark skin (at the time, the dark-skinned gypsies were called "Egyptians" from which the word gypsies is derived), and in the fifteenth century they proclaimed Sara their patron saint.

The festivities begin on Saturday when the *châsse*— a large silver-plated trunk containing the relics of saint Marie-Jacobé and saint Marie-Salomé—is slowly lowered from its niche high above the altar by means of cords and pulleys, while the feverish crowd below chants and awaits the relics with lighted candles. After nearly thirty minutes, the Châsse finally touches down and the gypsies throng forward to touch it with their candles, asking blessings and commending their children to the sainted Maries. Now it is Sara's turn. Her statue is brought up from the crypt of the church and first given a new dress. She gets a new dress every year which is put over her previous dresses, resulting in her curiously bulky appearance and disproportionately tiny head. Carried by chanting gypsies and preceded by a group of *Gardians* (the local cowboys on their white horses), Sara makes her way through town and to the beach. There, the statue-bearers, surrounded by the Gardians on horseback, walk their black madonna a few steps into the water to symbolize Sara's arrival by sea.

This ritual is repeated the next morning when the two Maries are carried to the sea after a high mass said by the archbishop of Aix-en-Provence. They are represented by two rather primitive-looking statues of one blond and one black-haired Marie, seated in a little boat that is carried through town on a dozen strong shoulders and is accompanied by beautiful Arlésiennes in traditional dress and the ever-present Gardians holding high their long tridents. When they arrive at the water's edge, the Gardians again walk their horses into the sea and flank the gypsies who wade waist-high into the waves carrying the holy Maries in their boat. The archbishop accompanies them in a fisherman's boat and blesses the sea, the town, the pilgrims and the gypsies. Loud chants of Ave, Ave, Ave Mariaaaa! welcome everyone back on shore and envelop the joyous procession on its way back to church where the holy Maries in their boat are reunited with black Sara.

The last ritual of this pilgrimage takes place that afternoon when the archbishop conducts a religious ceremony to celebrate the hoisting of the Châsse of relics back to the safety of its high lair above the altar. It is a moving moment, as the gypsies take this last chance to touch their candles to the silver Châsse and hold their children up to kiss it, all the while shouting prayers, and asking blessings and protection. Then they accompany Sara back to the crypt in an emotional farewell for another year. I knew a moment of panic when I followed the pilgrims into the crowded crypt where I found myself pressed against the wall and surrounded by burning candles which in the excessive heat had drooped into dripping fire hazards. Sara was watching, however, and kept us safe.

As a tourist one can't help but feel like a bit of an intruder in this private gypsy moment, yet these pilgrims seem to take us in stride and once the ceremonies are over and they return to their wagons, they quickly revert to stereotype by demanding money for picture taking or offering to read your palm. They are all there—the beautiful Esmeraldas with large loopy earrings, the standard-feature fortune tellers, the gruff menfolk and the begging children—the very picture of gypsydom. The nasty thought did cross my mind that this gypsy pilgrimage, which draws many tourists, might be an irresistible commercial opportunity. But then I remembered the fervor I had witnessed, the upturned tear-stained faces following the relics until they were out of sight, and the fact that these people had traveled thousands of miles to gather here once a year, as their forefathers had, to pay homage to their venerated Sara. This *has* to be real and I felt privileged to witness it.

A Scarred Beauty

Some say that perfect beauty is boring. Others believe that beauty is enhanced by an imperfection, which would serve to underline the excellence of the rest. Of course that would depend on the type of imperfection. The Venus of Milo without arms remains a thing of beauty, but Grace Kelly with a chipped front tooth just wouldn't do.

If beauty is in the eye of the beholder, my eyes found Aix-en-Provence beautiful at first sight. Human-sized with a well-preserved old city center, rich façades of an ochre-yellow local stone, sculpted fountains everywhere, the lush green canopy of the double rows of plane trees that line the splendid Cours Mirabeau and keep it cool in summer, abundant market stalls every day of the week, and an easygoing lifestyle to go with it all. Very nice indeed, but...

Yes, there is often a 'but' and Aix is no exception. With all its blessings and special attractions Aix is shamefully dirty. She is unkempt, like a beauty queen with dirty fingernails or greasy hair. She is tattooed with graffiti and soiled with dog poop and her streets are strewn with litter. Lack of municipal services? I don't think so.

Every evening the city's sanitation trucks empty the Dumpsters and trash cans dispersed throughout the center and pick up the plastic garbage bags that people place in front of their houses. In addition, every morning a city crew washes down the streets with powerful hoses, cleaning them of dog do and all evidence of nighttime revelry, and leaving them shimmering, albeit briefly, with cleanliness and freshness. But by mid-morning the streets have been reclaimed by thoughtless citizens who seem to have little concern for what they or their dogs leave behind. Few dog owners here seem to be familiar with pooper-scoopers and plastic bags, although one day I saw a beautifully dressed lady with a Louis Vuitton handbag from which dangled a tiny dogbone-shaped little purse that contained a few tightly rolled plastic bags. She had a small dog on a leash, one of those trembling miniature ones, who dropped some perfectly round pellet-like poops in front of my door. The lady was quick to pick them up with the purpose-built plastic bag, giving me an apologetic look. It was all so unusual that I almost said: "Oh, just leave them; they're adorable."

Deliveries are difficult in the narrow streets of the old center and as a rule they take place during the morning hours when restaurants and shops receive their supplies. This inevitably causes traffic back-ups, but the locals will try to avoid those hours and know how to take evasive action when they see a delivery truck down the street. However, when merchants receive their cartons they throw them out as soon as they are emptied but without flattening them, so that sidewalks are often blocked by heaps of carton boxes. It's an attitude: why bother if the garbage truck will pick them up and crush them?[1]

You can tell the arrival and departure of the city's 40,000 university students in late August and late May by the throwaways outside their rental housing. There are no dorms here, and when students move into their rented apartments the narrow sidewalks are clogged with boxes and packing materials, while at move-out time the clutter includes used mattresses, small refrigerators, lamps and anything else the students have judged not worth moving or keeping. Someone will clean it up, as always.

---

[1] In 2010 the City began testing a new service: on weekday afternoons a municipal pick-up truck will collect folded cartons from inner-city sidewalks.

Of course there are city ordinances against littering, but it is only too well known that they are never enforced. Last summer an article in the local newspaper proudly announced the formation of the Green Brigade, a sort of garbage police. This unit of four people is charged with catching and fining those who break the sanitation laws regarding trash disposal and dog feces removal. The Brigade needs to be sworn in since they will be giving tickets, and only two of the four members have been confirmed in their function so far. The wheels of city government do grind slowly. The Green Brigade article, which appeared more than a year after the first official listing of fines (€70 for 'dog ejections'), talked at length about the choice of uniforms. I can see us getting sidetracked here…

Living where we do, we not only have the usual inner-city street litter but also special lunchtime litter. We are plagued by stoopers—young people who take their lunches on our front steps. These high school students have no cafeteria and buy their lunches at take-out places, then settle down to eat on the steps of a nearby fountain or in a recessed doorway. Food wrappers, French fries and empty soda cans mark their passing—evidence that once again the nearest trash can was just beyond their reach.

Until recently we had an elderly next-door neighbor who fed the pigeons with the leftovers of her dinner which she would dump directly in the street. Splash! it went, every day. She saw no need for a bowl or a dish, which was a problem because the pigeons' menu was rich in sauce-covered pasta and half-chewed chicken bones. The area in front of her door was soon marked with permanent grease spots which even the city sanitation service could not clean off. I see it as a sort of grave marker to the old lady, who passed away this year. May she find a new flock of pigeons to feed in her next home.

Graffiti are part of many an urban setting and generally considered an eyesore, but years ago then-Minister-of-Culture Jack Lang declared them an artistic expression and a form of mainstream contemporary art. Some graffiti murals are indeed impressive, but this cannot be said for most of the pithy expressions that call out to us from walls and scaffolds. Even when they are not aggressive or obscene, how would you like to find "I'll walk to the moon and back for you babe" in dayglow spray paint across your façade? Removal of this type of paint, by sandblasting and/or chemical means, inevitably damages the old stone and leaves deep pits and gouges. Add acne to our city's blemishes.

Miraculously, the municipality somehow manages to clean up graffiti just before the touristy summer season. By the time the opera festival opens, most graffiti have disappeared from the walls in the old city and seem to have floated to the rooftops and other how-did-they-get-there places. I confess to a secret admiration for the one who risks his life to spray-paint graffiti hanging upside down from an attic window or a railway overpass, but I wouldn't want to be his mother.

Another well-oiled cleaning operation is the after-market show, a beautiful ballet between cleanup crews and café owners. Half an hour after the market stalls are taken down, the square is washed clean and café tables and chairs have taken their place. Not a stray tomato in sight, not a whiff of fish in the air. Where there's a will…

Garbage disposal is a difficult problem in the old center of Aix where most streets are too narrow for anything but small garbage cans and where little squares may have to choose between a trash bin and motorcycle parking. One such square, at the end of my street, tried to solve the problem by putting the bin underground, as is done on the Cours Mirabeau to accommodate the many restaurants, but as soon as the digging had begun the workmen hit some old remains and all work was stopped. Even though this time it was nothing precious from Roman times but rather some construction from Napoleonic days, the buried bin idea was dropped and the hole filled up again.

So what's to be done? Unless the city finally decides to levy the heavy fines it has threatened, I do not believe the French care enough to change their behavior. Yet, they are quick to show their solidarity on many levels and are among the most generous donors to disaster relief worldwide. They really do heed a call to their better instincts so perhaps a strong appeal to their civic duty and individual responsibility may be in order. I am hopeful, but I won't hold my breath.

In the meantime, I'll just keep practicing my Gallic shrug and try not to see the dirt.

Buying Wine

No matter where you live in France, there always seems to be a winery within easy driving distance. This is especially true in the wine areas of Bourgogne, Beaujolais, and Bordeaux, but also in the southern regions of Languedoc-Roussillon, Côtes du Rhône, and the Var, to mention only the ones I know.

If you have ever rented a summer house in these areas, it is likely that your village had a "coop" (pronounced co-op and short for *coopérative de vin*). This is the place where local growers take their grapes, to be mixed and pressed together with others and turned into an inexpensive red, white, or rosé wine. Most of these wines are non-varietal and are sold in bottles or in five- or ten-liter containers. The old-fashioned plastic containers have been replaced by today's practical vacuum packs with a built-in little faucet that allows you to fill a bottle or pitcher directly from the refrigerator where your wine is kept cool.

For young summer wines the coop is a good address, especially since this social drink is consumed in great quantities in summer. It's cheaper than mineral water, after all, and so much more satisfying on a shaded terrace or under a plane tree. A simple lunch of melon and prosciutto or cold charcuterie, salad, cheese and fruit begs to be accompanied by "un petit rosé" before you lie down for "une petite sieste." Don't feel guilty; everyone else does the same. Life in the village stops for lunch. Shop windows are shuttered and won't open again until 4:00 PM. (The same is true in the city, except for the department stores.) The mid-day summer hours of roughly 1:00 PM to 4:00 PM are considered too hot and unsuitable for work. And nobody, except perhaps mad dogs and Englishmen, would expect otherwise.

Commercial and other activity resumes after 4:00 PM and shops will then stay open until 7:00 PM or 8:00 PM, when it is time to sit down for an "apéro"—

the obligatory drinks and nibbles before dinner. There may be olives, cherry tomatoes, radishes, *tapenade* on toast, a dry sausage on a wooden cutting board with the traditional Opinel knife, or a *caillette* (a kind of pork paté), perhaps some cloves of garlic to be rubbed on bread with a bit of olive oil, and usually a local white or rosé wine. Pastis and perhaps a sweet walnut wine may also be offered, but no hard liquor as a rule.

This prelude to dinner is a good moment to compare notes on wines. Which coop this year? Any new finds? You may have your own addresses, refined over the years, but you always want to hear about new discoveries or recent improvements. *Goûte-moi ça* (taste this), says the host as he pours a foretaste of the red for the evening, *qu'en penses-tu?*—and you're on your way...

The coops have their place in the world of wine the way supermarkets have their use as food stores. But to find the lay-away wines for your *cave*, the better stuff for better meals, you must go the chateaux. And here is one of the great rewards of living in France. Driving through the lovely countryside to known and unknown chateaux is not just about buying wine. Some of the tasting rooms of these wineries are in indistinct sales offices, but others are found in beautiful settings that delight more than your palate. It's a joy to linger in the gardens of Val Joanis in Pertuis (Côtes du Luberon), and the beautiful view *en perspective* of the terraced lawns of Chateau de la Gaude (Côteaux d'Aix) is worth the trip.

And you always learn something. In driving through wine country you often see long low buildings with tiled roofs. When these roofs do not have the usual red tile color but have large blackened or purplish areas, you know that this is a distillery where *marc* (similar to *eau de vie* or *grappa*) is made, and the alcohol fumes have caused a fungus to grow in the roof.

A few years ago we discovered a little winery in Sarrians near Chateauneuf du Pape that has remained our all-time favorite. The third-generation winemaker was trying to run the business pretty much on his own then, dealing as best he could with a seriously ill wife and a teenage son still in school. He was open only on Saturdays and by appointment, and did no shipping (no time) and no advertising (no money). His well-established reputation was based on his wonderful full-bodied red, every bit as good as Chateauneuf du Pape but costing a fraction of the price.

Today, his wife is better, his son works by his side (and recently won second prize in a national sommelier contest), he is open six afternoons a week, and has added rosé to his repertoire. The rosé turned out to be very good and we added some to our order. He was pleased at our reaction and poured again, with a tiny note of caution: *Ça se boit facilement* (this one goes down easily). That's when I noticed the degree of alcohol on the label: a whopping 15 percent! I tried to envision the critics' notes; those who call wines witty, or mischievous or seductive—often more poetry than useful fact. And then I found it: this rosé was rollicking!

Douce France—
Strikes and All

When friends say they envy us for living in the south of France I sometimes feel like telling them that it is not all roses down here. (There, that should make them feel better). Take strikes, for example. As French as the *baguette* but a lot harder to digest, *la grève* is so regular an occurrence here that it has become part of the fabric of life. I was used to transportation strikes— airplanes, trains, buses, they all strike for reasons varying from *les 35 heures* (the shortened work week) to protests against violence (a bus driver gets beaten up by hooligans and before he can say *Ouch!* his fellow drivers have shut down the region's bus service), or requests for "danger pay" by those who feel their jobs warrant it, and on and on.

But we have also had a strike of tax collectors and a strike of driving inspectors. The latter struck because two inspectors in the Paris and Aix-en-Provence regions had been attacked by students they had failed (you used to get the results of your driving test right away; today it is sent to you by mail). The strike lasted about a month, causing back-ups and irritation at a time when high schools were getting out and many youngsters were scheduled to take their long-awaited tests before summer break. The tax inspectors shut the shop because the government had announced plans to consolidate the numerous existing tax-collecting offices into two main centers—one in the north and one in the south—which would obviously have put a number of people out of jobs. *NON, NON et NON!* was the response and after a month the government relented.

Another surprising one was the news strike. Of the three major news channels, two went on strike for over a week, leaving the third channel with 100 percent of the audience. The striking channels filled the airwaves with re-runs of Bennie Hill shows and Cagney and Lacey (remember them?). All in French of course, which makes Bennie Hill considerably less funny. The radio news of these channels also went on strike. If only no news were good news...

Recently, we had a strike by truck drivers who blocked several strategic highways and major access roads to protest against the high price of gasoline. Nothing surprising about that, except that the start of this strike was announced to begin on a Monday morning at nine o'clock, unusually late for maximum effect. The reason given was that the truckers wanted to avoid problems for high school students who that day were to start their final examinations nationwide at 9:00 AM. Nice thought. Thank you, truckers!

I have been living here long enough not to get excited about strikes any more, since they are always announced in advance and usually last only a couple of days. One summer, however, we had a strike that got everyone's attention and remains unresolved to this day: the strike by the *Intermittents du spectacle*—the temps of the theater world. These temps work only when called upon but have year-round salaries, covered by unemployment insurance. When the government announced planned cutbacks in this system, the reaction was swift and ferocious. The *Intermittents* shut down all the summer festivals, including Aix (opera) and Avignon (theater), with disastrous results for the local hotels and restaurants during their top season. But full-time pay for part-time work in theater has long been an acquired right in France, and the French cling to these *droits acquis* like barnacles to a boat.

It is always difficult to let go of something good and I suspect that elsewhere these acquired rights would not be given up without a fight either. However, the French have a tradition of settling their disputes in the street and this usually happens with overwhelming support of the citizens. Perhaps the reason for this is that France is a country of *fonctionnaires* (even cleaning people and cafeteria servers in schools are *fonctionnaires d'état*) and that every single one of them feels that the next cutback might happen to him. Be that as it may, the average Frenchman will not break a strike, and *solidarité* is de rigueur here. Charles de Gaulle is claimed to have said that a country with more than four hundred cheeses is ungovernable, and perhaps he was right.

———— • ————

Yet, in spite of it all, life remains *douce* here. Paid vacations are long (starting at thirty working days per year), retirement starts at age sixty for most and as early as fifty for some professions, and leisure time is generally valued more than an increased paycheck. When newly elected president Sarkozy urged his fellow citizens to work more in order to be paid more, most of them preferred to hold on to the thirty-five hours per week work schedule that had been imposed by an earlier, socialist government in order to create jobs.

The feared French bureaucracy turned out to be the mouse that roared. We found buying a house, a car, and obtaining a residency permit no more difficult or complicated here than elsewhere. We may agree that this country is overregulated, yet only in France is your driver's license issued for life! No renewal needed—ever. Inconsistent, it may seem, in a bloated bureaucracy, but perhaps this is just another example of *l'exception française.*

I don't know who first came up with the expression "Living like God in France." It does not say "Living like God in Byelorussia," so there seems to be some general agreement that living conditions are pretty good here. I can only agree.

Among the senior set, playing *boules* or *pétanque* is by far the most popular sport. And when you know that playing boules is about as exhausting as watching it, you can understand that many boules players are—'ow you say?—perhaps a bit hefty? Lots of pots out there. It's a sport for older guys who move slowly and talk a lot. And once they are finished moving slowly and talking a lot, they go to the café and play cards. In the center of Aix-en-Provence there is a *boulodrome* where you can still find a little sign that says "No Women." See if we care. But the other day they showed the world championship Pétanque in Marseilles on television and it was an altogether different thing. Young(ish) men in white trousers and tennis shoes, graceful fluid moves, lots of hits, and commented on television in the hushed tones that are usually reserved for Wimbledon center court matches. No need to get all sweaty, however. And no need to be a youngster either.

Every day, the weather reporter on television signs off with, "Today we celebrate St. Anne" or St. Paul or Victor or another saint. In this lay country, this has something appealingly traditional—like the almanac—about it. War and terrorism seem farther away, somehow.

And on Sunday morning, the most active place in town is still the pastry shop with its patient queue of customers, who would not think of coming home to Sunday lunch without the expected string-bound pastry box.

It isn't perfect, perhaps, but I think I'll stay.

Silkworms and Mistral

Have you ever heard of a *magnanerie*? It is a silk-worm nursery—a building dedicated to the rearing of silkworms (*magnans* in Provençal) on leaves of the mulberry tree until they are ready to spin their co-coons. In nineteenth-century France the raising of silkworms was primarily done by women (the *mag-nanarelles*), who during the second half of March carried the silkworm eggs, tied in a soft little bag, between their breasts to speed up their hatching. It was also the women who collected the mulberry leaves on which the silkworms fed themselves to bursting at least three times a day until, after four moultings, the fat grubs would finally begin to spin their cocoons. To harvest the silk, the cocoons were dropped in boiling water which would kill the chrysalis inside but also loosened the beginning of the silk thread which could then be carefully spooled.

Many farmers had a magnanerie in the attic of their *mas* or *bastide* to produce a small supplemental income. Others constructed two- or three-story build-ings specifically for the purpose of sericulture. Espe-cially in the Cévennes, these magnaneries flourished in the nineteenth century until the dreaded disease *pebrine* wiped out the entire silkworm population there in 1854 and effectively ended local sericulture. Louis Pasteur later found a cure for pebrine but it was too late for many magnaneries. Those that escaped the disease finally succumbed to the combined forces of artificial silk and massive imports from India. Today, magnaneries still dot the French landscape, but most have been converted to country inns or bed-and-breakfasts.

Like magnaneries, pigeon towers are a reminder of the old days when *pigeonniers* were built to house pigeons and collect their droppings for fertilizer. This rich fertilizer, called columbine, was so highly prized that it sometimes was part of a bride's dowry! In dried form it also was thought to cure baldness. These pigeonniers were abolished in the 1789 revolution as one of the hated privileges of the rich landowners whose pigeons fattened themselves on the grains and seed of tenant farmers' plots before ending up on the rich man's table. Sometimes freestanding, sometimes attached to a bastide, these round or rectangular pigeonniers usually had a *larmier*—a glazed tile moulding midway up the tower to prevent rats or cats from getting to the pigeons. Many pigeonniers have been preserved and today may serve as private residences. A particularly attractive one, converted to a home, can be found in the village of Lourmarin.

Another pretty sight in towns and villages throughout Provence is the open bell towers. The iron-framework steeples of these bell towers were left open so that the mistral, that hard-blowing dry wind from the north, can pass through them. The typical Provençal *mas* (farmhouse) always faces south, its blind-walled back turned to the mistral. The much-maligned mistral, which according to local lore blows either three, six, or nine days in a row, has been blamed for everything from migraines to insanity and suicide, partly because it blows without letup. Apparently, nine days of howling mistral can be beyond human endurance.

Our winter weather is generally mild except when the mistral blows icy air from the northwest through the Rhône valley and chills us to the bone. One of the most popular *Santons* at Christmas time is the shepherd, leaning into the wind holding on to his floppy hat while the mistral blows his long coat up behind him. No Provençal crèche is without this wind-fighting shepherd. In the center of town, surrounded by churches and other tall structures, we suffer less than those in the countryside and simply turn up the heating a notch. It doesn't happen often and, after all, the mistral is part of where we live.

The mistral can blow at any time of the year and is particularly feared in summertime, when it can fan a minor spark or a poorly extinguished cigarette into a devastating forest fire that is extremely hard to put out. Particularly in the coastal area of the Var, where the mistral is channeled in easterly direction through forested mountain ranges at up to ninety km. an hour, hardly a summer goes by without some major fire and often loss of property and life.

Yet, we can thank the mistral for the famous light of the south, so beloved by artists, and for our sunny, dry climate. After the passage of the mistral the skies are intensely blue and the air clean and pure. Pollution has been blown away and nature is sparkling and dust free. Air quality, especially around the oil refinery plant near Marseilles, is improved and we silently thank the mistral for its latest house-cleaning visit.

Village Life

A couple of months ago, I drove to a pretty little village in the Vaucluse to photograph for an American friend a property that was for sale there. When I had a hard time locating the exact address I stopped the car and asked a man dressed in the farmer's cornflower-blue overall for directions. He stepped back and checked out my (local) license plate before answering. It was a natural reflex, and once he had assured himself that I was local enough to be trusted he was kind and helpful. I should drive in the direction of that church over there on the hill, he indicated, and then follow the overhead electric wires for another kilometer or so.

Fifteen minutes later I found myself facing a fork in the road and unsure which branch to follow, so I decided to ask a nearby man on a tractor, explaining that someone in the lower village had directed me up here. Again, my license plate was inspected before he signaled me to follow his tractor to the place we were looking for. After a few hundred meters he made a sharp left turn and stopped in front of a small house where a woman was watering her front yard. He spoke to her, pointing to us, and a few moments later Madame wiped her hands on her housedress and came over to suggest that we leave the car there. The house we were looking for was nearby but invisible from the street, she explained, and she offered to walk us over. On our short walk she asked us if this was for ourselves? (I thought it prudent to say Yes); where did we live now?; did we have children?; would we live here year-round?; and suddenly I felt that these people had accompanied us the way your designated guide Olga used to accompany you in Moscow in the days of the USSR. Helpful, yes, but watchful even more.

Traditionally, peasants in these villages are suspicious, and this place was no exception. "What do they want here?" they seem to wonder; "let them go elsewhere." Foreigners were to be avoided, if possible, or at least left to their own devices: "Don't count on any help from us; we don't like *étrangers* here," which may mean foreigners, Parisians, or even people from another *département*. Images of *Jean de Florette* and *Manon des Sources* came into my head. I saw peasants banding together against my American friends, pitchforks at the ready, bent on protecting the sanctity of their village, and suddenly the dreamed-of "house in Provence" was a lot less attractive. At least in this corner.

French villages do have their charm, however. Clustered around a chateau on a hill or nestled in a valley and surrounded by a quilt of brightly colored fields, they can be picture-postcard pretty. The church, the *Mairie*, and the *café* were the beating heart of the old village that lived from farming, where local sons married local daughters, and where the mailman would have his first *pastis* at the village bar during his morning round. But today, tourism is changing the picture, and little restaurants, boutiques, souvenir shops, or even art galleries are cropping up and houses are being renovated all over.

Old habits die hard, however, and in the evenings the older villagers still move their kitchen chair outside and lean back against the wall to watch the comings and goings for a while, their solid wives by their side, as they have always done. They largely keep to themselves and to their old ways, even if around them the world is changing. "Just imagine," they'll tell each other, "houses being bought and renovated, to be used only a few weeks a year. No good can come of this."

One year we rented a house in such a village for our summer vacation. Coming out into the garden the first day, I saw the neighbor, an elderly peasant, who was watering his large garden full of fruit trees with a simple watering can. Wiry and bent over, his face shaded by a straw hat, he passed me as he worked his way back to the house and I said Hello to him. He barely lifted his head, spit a grunt at me, and continued his watering. As time went by he seemed to soften somewhat and by the end of two weeks he managed to nod his head in greeting. We had come a long way and were almost on speaking terms. I learned later that the owner of our house and this peasant had had an unresolved dispute years ago. In typical village fashion—never forgive, never forget.

Just like two branches of the same family who ran the two grocery stores in this village. Generations ago, a family dispute had caused a rift that remained as wide today as ever, and even though their shops were located on the same street, practically across from each other, the respective owners refused to bury the hatchet and kept a flinty eye on each other at all times. Memories are long here, and grudges run deep.

At the same time, villagers will always protect each other against outsiders. This popular and touristy village had a village idiot—let's call him JoJo—a man in his forties who lived with his father and a little dog. Their old house, just in back of the main street, was one of the few to have a balcony. The garden of the house we rented was within earshot of this balcony, where JoJo would sit on summer evenings with his instruments. As soon as he heard voices—of outdoor diners and their guests—he would start blowing warning blasts on his trumpet. When we stopped talking the trumpet would stop, but as soon as we resumed our conversations so would JoJo, this time switching to a "cacerolazo"—banging metal spoons on pots and pans as in Argentine street demonstrations. JoJo turned out to be totally intolerant of noise, even quiet table talk some thirty feet away, and we had no choice but to whisper or go back inside. Other neighbors had long ago given up reasoning with JoJo and accepted his bizarre behavior with a Gallic shrug. *"Il est nerveux, Madame"* was all there was to it. JoJo might be an idiot, but he was *their* idiot.

Weddings

When a French friend invited us to the wedding of her daughter that was to take place at the family chateau, we were delighted to accept and travel to "their" village of one hundred souls. It would be an opportunity to visit a new "*département,*" catch up with a few old friends, and celebrate a joyous occasion. We made an overnight stop at the lovely medieval village of Cliousclat in the Drôme, where several families have been potting for generations. Like Vallauris in the Var, where Picasso potted, Cliousclat has good clay which has been used for pottery for over three centuries. The next morning, we visited several potters and found a lovely ceramic bowl for the bride.

Another two hours' driving through beautiful countryside brought us to our destination where we found the little church all scrubbed and decked out in flowers by the village women. After the 6:00 PM mass and before we settled down to a candlelit dinner at the chateau, a reception was held in the street to which all the villagers were invited. As we were standing around with our champagne I noticed the local obelisk, the poignant "*monument aux morts pour la patrie 1914–1918.*" Every village has one and, as always, it told an awful story. Of the one hundred local inhabitants, eleven died in this war and among those eleven there were three sets of brothers.

The village consists of tenant farmers who farmed the chateau's vast lands for many generations. But the *chatelain* has been selling off houses and land over time and today can barely keep up the chateau which is sliding into disrepair. I had the feeling I was witnessing the end of an era. The lord is dying, the serfs are leaving and their houses are being bought by foreigners. It appears that two English families have already settled in this tiny village, as have so many others throughout Provence and the Dordogne. Soon the houses will be equipped with hot and cold running water, the outdoor plumbing will be moved indoors, and the village will slowly take on a different look and character. And a new life as well.

These days, old villages no longer die; they get "saved" by foreigners who seek second homes and are happy to restore the crumbling houses and install swimming pools. The village elders are happy too, since they have never had so much money in their life and can now afford to build a little house outside the village with some modern amenities. I still remember the woman who cleaned the house we used to rent in Lourmarin. When her husband died, she sold their old house on the main street and bought a smaller one in a new development on the outskirts where she was very proud to show us her washing machine—the first one she had ever owned.

In Aix-en-Provence we sometimes "attend" several weddings a week. Even though we are mere onlookers, it is hard not to participate, even peripherally, in some wedding activity around City Hall. Every Saturday morning the flower market is set up on the *Place de la Mairie* in front of the beautiful eighteenth-century city hall with its charming cobblestoned courtyard. As soon as the flower stalls are taken down at 1:00 PM and the nearby cafés have put their tables and chairs back outside, the first of the brides arrives. People stop and smile at the bride and groom as they move into the courtyard with their entourage where they wait to be called into the *Salle des Marriages*, there to be joined in civil matrimony by the Mayor.

Usually, this ceremony takes no more than half an hour, but schedules have a way of being approximate here, especially when you consider that the famous "*quart d'heure aixois*" allows the locals to feel that they are on time when they walk in fifteen minutes late. This goes for the mayor as well. So when the first bride and groom come back out into the courtyard, the second bridal party is already waiting there and ready to exchange places before the mayor. Outside, on the *Place de la Mairie*, a third bride has taken up her place in line, being photographed and admired by bystanders. I once witnessed a back-up of three brides when the official car of a departing bride turned out to be blocked by an illegally parked motorcycle and the party was trapped until the police intervened. It turned into an occasion for the three brides to meet and kiss and encourage each other, and for a nearby bar owner to rush over with a bottle of champagne. The mother of the "stuck" bride, not at all put out, kept singing "*J'ai marié ma fille! J'ai marié ma fille!*" and turning dangerous pirouettes on her stiletto heels. The crowd cheered, tourists snapped pictures, and soon the bridal holding pattern dissolved when the next group was called in by the mayor.

A House in Provence

Provence today is equated with the good life. Good climate and good food in a beautiful setting—just what the doctor ordered. But so many foreigners have followed in Peter Mayle's wake after *A Year in Provence* appeared more than twenty years ago that it has become increasingly difficult and expensive to find a good house in the area today. Moreover, the advent of the high-speed TGV train to Avignon, Aix-en-Provence and Marseilles has added a new element to the buyers' pool: executives from Paris and Lyons who choose to work from a home office in the milder south in exchange for a weekly commute to their headquarters.

So as supply dwindles and prices increase, village houses are being restored and turned into boutiques and art galleries, while the falling-down old *bastide* in the countryside—the ideal fixer-upper—is hardly priced at fixer-upper levels, especially in dollar terms. Besides, a fixer-upper in Provence is not for everyone and can be not only a strain on your wallet but also on your patience and your tolerance for coping with repeated delays and their imaginative explanations. I know of one case where at the end of a torturous renovation process, the house-in-Provence was finally ready for occupancy but the owners were no longer able to agree on anything, including their marriage. The house was sold, the proceeds divided, and the couple went their separate ways. There is not always a happy ending.

Better, perhaps, to look at new housing, a category that is in full bloom and gives no sign of slowing down. Many new developments (called *lotissements* here) have been built near popular cities or around golf courses and marinas. With easy access to airports and TGV stations, these gated communities can be attractive to foreign buyers who worry about security in their absence, and who can avail themselves of local management to rent out their house or apartment on demand. Most of these, however, bear little resemblance to the *bastide* or country house amidst lavender and olive trees that you may have seen in your travels or read about in *Town & Country*. Here, practicality, security and return-on-investment come first.

Not so long ago, however, Provence was among the poorest areas of France. Mostly agricultural, it scratched a living from poor land, weathered recurring droughts, floods, phylloxera and other natural disasters, and desperately fought to hold on to its *terroir* from generation to generation—until in the mid-1960s the newly built Canal de Provence brought irrigation and relief to the Provençal farm. The farmer had learned to be frugal, however; he ate what he grew or killed, and wasted nothing. Ears, feet, snouts, tongues, cheeks, tripes, intestines—it all went into the pot and with prolonged, slow cooking turned into the delicious fare that chefs are proud to feature on restaurant menus today. A wonderful Provençal stew, for instance, starts with the cheapest and toughest cuts of beef such as *jarret* or *joues de boeuf,* and after seven to eight hours of slow cooking in lots of red wine, becomes the much-prized *Daube de Boeuf* you can cut with a fork. During hunting season *marcassin* (young boar) may replace the beef. In fact, hunting used to supplement many a family's meals and had little to do with sport. The only meat you ate was the one you hunted and fortunately the area did not lack for game or fowl.

Another dish of humble origins is *Bouillabaisse,* the pride of Marseillais cuisine. Initially, this dish was made with the leftovers of the daily fish market: heads, net-damaged or unsellable fish, bits and pieces that were good only for a stew or a soup for the fishermen themselves. Over time, through the clever combination of flavors from certain firm rock fish and those from more delicate softer fish, a simple fish soup evolved into the savory dish known as bouillabaisse, served with *roux* and toasted bread, that is found in good fish restaurants all along the coast. The required combination is quite specific, however, and purists insist that an authentic bouillabaisse must contain at least seven or eight out of about a dozen selected types of fish. Any serious chef will therefore require twenty-four hours' notice for bouillabaisse so that the different prescribed varieties of fish can be bought fresh that morning. Ironically, the declining fish population in the Mediterranean and the great popularity of this dish have turned the humble bouillabaisse into one of the most expensive items on the menu today.

The hard-scrabble days are gone for good. Tourism and an exploding real-estate market have been pouring money into the south, and with it the usual changes for the better and the worse—better roads, faster trains, more airports, but bigger crowds, higher prices, less space, and more noise. Quiet is nearby, however, for those who seek it. Three Cistercian monasteries within easy driving distance from Aix-en-Provence—Silvacane, Senanque and Thoronet—three havens of peace and austere beauty, await you for a quiet visit, a stroll through the cloister, a concert, or a Sunday morning mass with Gregorian chants.

If you don't feel like driving, take a quiet evening stroll in Aix at sundown, after the shops are closed, and enjoy some things you may have missed during the daytime bustle on the *Place de la Mairie*, such as the huge wooden doors of City Hall with their magnificent carved lion heads which are easy to overlook during the day when the doors are open. Then look up to the pediment above the old post office (a former granary) to your left and discover a large male and female figure, representing the Rhône and the Durance rivers, amid sheaves of wheat and a cornucopia of grapes and fruits in a display of nature's bounty. The rubenesque Durance leans seductively against the Rhône while dangling her bare leg outside the pediment and over the cornice, jutting away from the façade. It is a sexy and humorous gesture of wellbeing, spontaneous and free, and perfectly in tune with today's pleasure-seeking ways. Provence is still, or again, a good place to be.

Surprising Marseilles

Among the many discoveries we made in Provence, Marseilles was perhaps the most surprising one. Like most foreigners, we had only a vague idea of Marseilles and a negative one at that. Movies like *The French Connection* as well as a number of crime reports in newspapers had given us the impression of a dangerous city, one where you carefully stayed within the well-trodden *Vieux Port* and went perhaps on a boat ride to one of the nearby islands, purse tightly clutched to your chest. It was not until we made friends in Marseilles that we got to know the city and came to love it.

In my opinion, the bad reputation of Marseilles as a mafia hotbed is no more deserved than the bad reputation of Washington, D.C., as "murder capital of the world." A grain of truth, regularly watered by bad press, has bloomed into a distorted image of both cities. Marseilles is a port city and as such a place of transit for drugs, illegal immigration, and—inevitably, it seems—a certain criminal element. *Le grand banditisme* we sometimes read about is the type of organized crime that robs Brinks trucks and wages war with rival criminals for the control of juicy markets such as gambling and drugs. Certainly, these are not choir boys, but the average tourist would be hard pressed to catch a glimpse of these heavies or get in the way of their territorial battles.

Therefore, it is not only safe but highly recommended to visit the wonderful *Vieux Port* of Marseilles that serves today as yacht harbor and departure point for boat trips to the *calanques* and the islands. Its opening to the sea is flanked by two forts, the Fort St. Jean of twelfth-century origin but expanded and fortified by Louis XIV in 1670, and on the opposite side the Fort St. Nicolas, built ten years later by Louis XIV to control the rebellious city. A good introduction to Marseilles would be to climb the stairs of the Fort St. Jean tower for a beautiful panoramic view, before walking the entire periphery of the Vieux Port to Fort St. Nicolas, past City Hall, the Tourist Office, the fish market (in the morning) and numerous outdoor cafés. You have now smelled the sea, heard the Marseillais accent, and felt the laid-back ambience of the place. You are ready to go exploring.

Our first surprise was that Marseilles has thirty-five miles of coastline, running from L'Estaque at the north end to Les Goudes at the south, and a number of islands just off shore. Driving along the Corniche Président Kennedy towards the *Parc Balnéaire du Prado*—an area of beaches, bicycle paths, swimming pools, volleyball fields, windsurfing—you are now about midway between the Vieux Port and Les Goudes, a tiny fishing village which for all its remoteness from the center is in fact in the eighteenth *arrondissement* of Marseilles. Soon after Les Goudes the paved road ends, you park your car and walk a few hundred meters towards Cap

Croisette which closes the Gulf of Marseilles and to the steep steps cut into the rocks down to the well-hidden *Baie des Singes*. You have come to finisterra—the end of the earth—and the most spectacular view of the blue infinity of the Mediterranean. Here the water is transparently turquoise and because of its remoteness the quietest piece of Mediterranean you are likely to swim in. Just a stone's throw away is a tiny rocky island without any visible vegetation that nevertheless sustains a small herd of wild goats. When I saw a she-goat and her kids walking along the crest I thought myself in ancient Greece—yet, I was still within the city limits of Marseilles!

Driving back along the coast toward the Vieux Port, we spotted the archipelago of Frioul and its little island of If made famous by Alexandre Dumas, whose Count of Monte Cristo was imprisoned in the notorious fortress-prison of *Chateau d'If*. We stopped for a minute at *Le Vallon des Auffes*, another seaside neighborhood of Marseilles, built around a small inlet lined with colorful little houses and bobbing with brightly painted *pointus*, the typical little fishing boats so named because they are pointed fore and aft. This little Vallon also houses *Chez Fonfon*, a fish restaurant that is known far beyond Marseilles for its bouillabaisse.

Back in the Vieux Port and turning our back to the Mediterranean, we walked to the nearby Roman Docks museum with its multitude of ancient amphora found on shipwrecked Roman galleons off Marseilles, and not far from one of my favorite parts of town, *Le Panier*. This hilly and densely populated poor neighborhood is rapidly being gentrified and is home to the most beautiful historic site in town, *La Vieille Charité*—a seventeenth-century hospice housed in a quadrangle of three-story arcaded galleries that surround a magnificent chapel with an unusual elliptical dome, the entire complex transformed into a museum in the 1970s. Lines of laundry span the narrow streets of Le Panier and remind you of Naples, while the pockets of Arabic heard here and there speak of the Maghreb and its many immigrants that poured into France by way of Marseilles.

Taking the stairs down the steep streets of Le Panier, we passed a little chocolate shop that seemed very popular. It turned out that there was space for only three or four people inside, so others awaited their turn outside. The place could not have been simpler—a little family business with a recipe for chunky blocks of dark chocolate that made addicts of its customers. According to a friend, here was the best orange-zest-laced dark chocolate in the world, even though the packaging left a bit to be desired. No pretty pralines here, not even a nice little box. A simple white paper bag is what you got, and either the shop owner would cut the block in pieces for you here or you took a hammer to it at home.

Another few blocks took us back to the Vieux Port where we decided to take a rest at one of the outdoor cafes. Looking up from our pastis we found the Basilica of *Notre-Dame-de-la-Garde*, built on a hill high above the port. There, on top of the steeple stands the gold-painted statue of *La Bonne Mère*, as she is affectionately called by the Marseillais, to watch over the nearly one million citizens below and the sailors out at sea, over the forty-five thousand students of the *Université de Marseille*, and the countless immigrants who came to find work here and ended up staying, creating their own neighborhoods and markets. She sees the ultra-modern silent tram gliding through the city streets; the glass expanse of the renovated St. Charles railway station whence a monumental carved stairway deposits travelers one hundred and four steps below onto La Canebière, the once very chic hotel-lined artery leading directly to the Vieux Port; the busy passenger port with its *va-et-vient* of ferryboats and cruise ships; the industrial port with its cargo ships and container docks; the sixty-thousand-seat stadium for football-mad Marseilles; the *calanques*, those beautiful fjord-like inlets carved by the sea into the tall limestone cliffs—and she knows that she is guarding a blessed place.

Naples having lost much of its luster in recent years no longer is the must-see city before dying. Marseilles is an excellent candidate, I think. Take a twenty-minute boat ride from the island of Frioul at sunset and watch in awe as the multi-hued city approaches, offset against its mountainous background, turning pink and opening its welcoming arms as you glide between the two forts into the Vieux Port, admire the scintillating *Bonne Mère* high above on your right and the beautiful City Hall on your left that so miraculously escaped the German bombs in World War II when all buildings around it were flattened. When the boat drops you off on the Quai des Belges, don't—please don't—leave until you have seen the lights come on and hold your breath in admiration at the sight of the two forts, the *Mairie*, the entire Vieux Port and of course *La Bonne Mère* illuminated in a magnificent glow against the night sky. Then see if you don't agree with me: see Marseilles and die.

Summer Festivities

Summer is festival season in the south, notably in Aix (opera), Avignon (theater), La Roque d'Anthéron (piano), Orange (opera), Marciac (jazz), Lacoste, Antibes, Nice, etc., and churches, cloisters and abbeys throughout France are home to concerts of all kinds. In summer this area fairly vibrates and swings with music old and new (in today's French *"ça vibre et ça swingue"*). Just imagine that the Avignon Festival, which was founded more than 60 years ago by actor-director Jean Vilar in the *Cour d'Honneur* of the Palace of the Popes, today counts about one thousand "In" and "Off" productions in numerous locations all over town, performed all day and throughout the evening for the entire month of July.

Needless to say, these festivals bring in thousands of visitors from all over the world. The University of Aix-Marseilles has cleverly tapped into this foreign influx by organizing *Les Rencontres Economiques d'Aix-en-Provence* in mid-Festival during three days in July. These conferences are open to the public, and we attended one on Globalization with keynote speaker Joseph Stiglitz, American Nobel-Prize winner for Economics, where we noticed among the attendees some familiar faces in government (such as Hubert Védrine, Bernard Kouchner, Alain Juppé, Dominique Strauss-Kahn, and Jack Lang) whom we might see again in the evenings at the opera.

It's not all high culture, however, as shown in many of the villages around us where summer celebrations are folksy and fun. In Saint-Rémy-de-Provence, for instance, they hold a *Feria* in mid-August, where cowboys from the Camargue compete in groups of five in running a small herd of bulls through the streets and trying not to lose one (this is called an "abrivado"). On their white horses they form a V-formation, one guy up front and the other four on either side behind him flanking about four bulls. The young men from Saint Rémy, out to show their courage and impress the girls, try to grab the last bull by the tail and separate him from the herd. The separated bull then has to be caught and brought back by a cowboy, but not before he has run wild through a screaming crowd. At one point, I was standing in a parking lot when a bull got loose and ran onto the lot where I was. There were cars and trucks that blocked my view but the screams told me he was near, and when he turned up again it really was too close for comfort. I cannot honestly say that I looked the bull in the eye but I was close enough to feel his spit! *Quelle aventure!*

The whole event is very colorful, with lots of folklore—Arlésiennes in open coaches, cowboys with long cattle prods dressed in Provençal shirts, paso doble music everywhere—and at the end of it all the prize for the best *manade* (cattle ranch), i.e. the group that lost the fewest bulls. Then, more music, dancing, and drinking to another happy ending.

In Lourmarin they celebrate their *Fête du Village* the last weekend of August. The itinerant *forains*, who have come a long way since the days of the wooden wagons, set up a three-day fair. Today, they have their wheeled houses pulled by Mercedeses, and as soon as they set up "camp" near the village green, their fancy gleaming caravans unfold front porches, balconies, and satellite dishes. Then the washing machine is rolled out onto the porch and for the next three days, their laundry on the line becomes part of the local landscape. They run various carnival attractions such as bumper cars, shooting galleries, merry-go-rounds, roulette tables, and sell chi-chis, churros and other fatty fare. And, of course, they play music, including tango and *paso doble*, which is always a great success with the older crowd. The women get dressed up, high heels and all, and dance with each other if their men-folk won't move. And Oscar and I dance the tango as best we can on gravel.

But one year a special effort was made to get the younger generation interested, so after the usual gypsy band we got a special show. A cart was rolled onto the stage (the kind they use at airports to move luggage onto the plane) with half a dozen creatures in wetsuits and diving gear. Then, to the sounds of the James Bond movie theme, they started peeling off their masks and flippers and put on sunglasses. When the lead guy began singing into his flipper and the two back-up girls started undulating, I knew we were in for a treat. I am not sure the older villagers knew what hit them and I suspect they would just as soon stick to the tango, but you can't stop progress.

The village of Maillane holds an age-old celebration of the wheat harvest which begins with a mass said in Provençal and the blessing of the traditional *Charette*, a huge four-wheeled farm cart decorated with flowers and greenery and pulled by about twenty horses. Each of the horses is also decorated with flowers and with a round bread tied to its halter, and is "walked" by a local youth who holds a costumed Arlésienne by the

hand. First, the whole cortège parades through the village with the statue of St. Eloi (it's his name day). Then the saint goes back to his church, the Arlésiennes withdraw, and the "race" begins—the young men holding the horses by their halters start running until the entire string of twenty horses with the cart at the end seems to be in full gallop, tearing by within inches of your face. The driver of the *charette* had a couple of children with him and seemed to be having a hard time keeping his wheels on the ground in the turns. But, apparently, there has never been an accident, and this time again everything ended well.

Around the same time, the village of Le Puy Sainte Réparade celebrates its *Fête du Pois Chiche*, the chickpea! Yes, the lowly chickpea has its own festival, which shows you that nothing is too insignificant for a day-long celebration here. As so often, the party starts in church where the village priest blesses all involved (people, animals and chickpeas) and a Provençal fife-and-tambourine band escorts the procession from the church to the main square where the games begin.

First, a hay wagon arrives, stacked high with chick-peas in the raw. For those who, like me, don't know whether chickpeas grow on trees or in the field, it is a surprise to see what looks like small smooth walnuts on dry, leafless twigs. These get dumped on a large canvas drop cloth laid out for this purpose. Next comes a big draught horse (I thought I recognized Hannibal from Villelaure), pulling a heavy stone roller. His handler guides him to the mass of chickpeas-on-branches on the canvas and, slowly and efficiently, Hannibal drags his roller over the piles and reduces them to broken bits and pieces. Now, an ancient-looking machine is pulled up, with a funnel-like top and a receptacle attached to its side. Two men heap the bits and pieces into the funnel, someone turns a handle, and the machine starts shaking and clattering and spitting "de-twigged" and unshelled chickpeas into the receptacle. The shells and twigs are removed and hauled away on the hay wagon, and the chickpeas are collected in baskets, to be given away later.

Now the canvas is rolled up, the wine starts flowing, and lunch is served in the *Salle des Fêtes* where long tables are set up for a giant Aïoli, the traditional cod fish dish, with chickpeas of course. The whole village is there, kids and dogs included, and those who are still sober after lunch get a chance to take a ride on Hannibal's back. Last time I looked, I saw a little grandmother in Provençal dress bobbing precariously on top of the huge gentle beast, her bonnet askew and her face aglow, screaming "Regardez, regardez!" the way we used to call out "Look at me, Mom!" The village band kept the good times rolling until dusk, Hannibal returned to his daily drudge, and I went home having learned the dark little secret of the chickpea.

You Are What You Eat

Am I really? Would that make me a criminal if I ate protected species? Or game outside hunting season? Or an overfished species that is trying to replenish itself? I may have to plead guilty here, but if ignorance counts I hope to be forgiven once again.

There was this invitation, you see. Parisian friends with a house in Provence invited us one evening to dinner in an out-of-the-way place and suggested that we meet at their house and drive out together. They explained that this place is not often open and that a reservation is hard to get, but they never mentioned the restaurant by name. I could not help thinking of great chefs and Michelin stars, but dropped that idea when we began slowing down on an unlit country road without the slightest sign of life, let alone a starred restaurant. Our driver kept throwing high beams and low beams on the road until he found the name he was looking for—painted on a small stone on the side of the road and barely visible. He tapped three short blasts on his horn and a man with a dog came out to meet us. "Park over there and follow me," he said, and opened the door into his kitchen, ordering the dog to stay outside.

We found ourselves in a large farmhouse kitchen with a long table and a huge fireplace where several big skewers were waiting to be positioned for slow cooking over the flames. There were six of us and the lone table was set for six. Our friends seemed to know the score and settled in for apéritifs of olives, *pâté,* and *tapenades,* country bread, and carafes of red and white wine. We ate, we drank and were merry while the owner busied himself in skewering various things on big skewers. When the dog barked, he stopped, picked up his flashlight and stepped outside to investigate. A minute later he came back, saying it was nothing but locking the door just the same. My table mates continued their conversation and the cook went back to his skewers. Soon, some vegetables were brought to the table as well as some slices of bread with meat drippings. Then appeared a large oval platter with what looked like a dozen little birds. They had been decapitated, plucked and roasted whole over the fire, their intestines intact to give additional flavor, and their juices caught on thick slices of bread. Everyone was served and a second platter soon replaced the first one. I was instructed on how to eat these birds, with my fingers, bones and all. Crisp and brittle and very flavorful, each little bird was only a few mouthfuls, and the bones seemed no harder than a thin bread stick. This was a delicacy that was sinfully good—a description more accurate than I realized at the time.

Once safely in the car on our way back, our friends told me that we had dined on little thrushes, shot illegally during their migration. The "restaurant" was the house of a *braconnier,* a poacher, who was known to a select circle of gourmets who had no qualms about paying handsomely for this forbidden fruit. I felt as if I had eaten my canary, but soon let my guilt feelings evaporate in the face of my ignorance and the food fetish of my friends.

On another occasion we joined some friends in an early-evening swim just outside Marseilles. We were told to bring our bathing suits as well as a baguette and some white wine because we might fish something. As it turns out, this lovely secluded spot was known to our Marseillais friends as a place where *oursins* (sea urchins) could be found. A couple of exploratory dives confirmed that there were indeed plenty of urchins there and when we came up for air we picked up the rubber gloves and nets we had brought for this purpose and dove again. The sea urchins seemed to be sitting on rocks or lying underfoot just a couple of meters below sea level, ready to be picked up and put in our netty bags and hauled to the surface. Some of our friends knew how to dislodge the spiny urchins with a fork and their bare hands without getting hurt, but I preferred to use my rubber gloves. For all my trouble, I was not stung by any urchins but by a jelly fish on my way up.

After an hour of swimming and diving we had collected about a dozen urchins per person and decided it was time for our *apéritif*. We cut some bread, opened the white wine, and standing in the surf cut open the urchins with scissors, rinsed them in the sea and threw back the empty tops. We put the fresh urchins in their half shell on an improvised tray, to be scooped out with a piece of bread and washed down with wine—a delicious ultra-fresh gift from the sea. An hour later, as the sun was setting and we got dressed, we repaired to a nearby restaurant for a bit of seafood to round off our dinner. There, someone mentioned that we had actually beaten the season by one day, explaining that the official season for urchin fishing started tomorrow, the first of September. Yes, technically we had broken the law, but it was awfully difficult to feel guilty.

The Light

France in general, and Provence in particular, has always attracted artists. They came, they saw the light, they stayed and talked their fellow artists into joining them. We know that Vincent van Gogh settled in Arles and persuaded his friend Paul Gauguin to join him there (even though it destroyed their friendship), that Matisse and Picasso chose the Riviera, as did Marc Chagal who settled in St. Paul de Vence. Living in the south was cheap then and the climate pleasant.

But the visual arts were not the only art that flourished in the south, where writers felt the pull as well. Robert Louis Stevenson spent enough time in the Cévennes to write his *Travels with a Donkey* there; M.F.K. Fisher wrote about her years in Aix-en-Provence and Marseilles; Lawrence Durrell settled in Sommières (and died there) where he wrote his Avignon Quintet; Argentine writer Julio Cortazar had a little house in Saignon in the Vaucluse, where he lived whenever he could get away from Paris and his work as a translator for Unesco; Aldous Huxley had a house in Sanary-sur-Mer and Edith Wharton owned a place in Hyères; Graham Greene lived in Nice for many years, and Somerset Maugham spent most of his life in Cap

Ferrat where he produced the bulk of his work. American artist Gerald Murphy and his wife Sara received and nurtured an amorphous colony of artists at their Villa America in Antibes and inspired the likes of Dorothy Parker, Scott Fitzgerald, Ernest Hemingway, Archibald Macleish, and John Dos Passos to set some of their novels in the south of France.

There are other beautiful places in the world, so what is it about this area that so inspires artists? I don't believe hedonism is the answer because fun in the sun gets old very quickly and might even run counter to the solitude that any serious artistic effort requires. Of course the climate and the beauty of the place contribute to a sense of general wellbeing, but in the end I believe the answer is to be found in the particular luminosity of Provence.

If it is true that Sweden's high number of suicides is directly related to the lack of daylight during its long winters, then an abundance of light might have the opposite effect. Yet we never hear about the salutary effect of light in, say, Africa or Spain or other sun-soaked countries. So if sun is not the answer, could it be the wind?

The mistral, that is, the infamous north-south wind of Provence that can blow for days on end and is reputed to have driven men mad. Granted, it has its bad side. While it blows, the mistral is unpleasant, but think of it as the proverbial toothache that feels great when it stops. That's when its good side shows, because in its wake it leaves skies so clear and so intensely blue as to be almost unnatural. It's a deep Matisse blue, without a smudge of cloud, and of such crystal clarity that you can see forever. Or at least to Corsica. Pollen and other impurities are gone for a while and everything looks bright and freshly buffed. I can just see Cézanne, who painted mostly outdoors, happily setting up his easel again before the newly scoured Montagne Sainte Victoire in search of yet another variation of light and shape in its craggy stoniness. And I am again stopped in my tracks when I look up at the open bell towers that are sharply outlined against these bright-blue skies such as I have never seen anywhere else.

If I were a painter, I know that this would make me reach for my brush. As it is, I just take in the abundance of color all around me—from the ochre-colored soil to the silvery-green olive orchards, from the pine-covered mountains to the turquoise waters of the *calanques*, from the straight-lined rows of blooming lavender to the buttery fields of rape seed—and I reach for my pen, while quietly rejoicing in my good fortune of living in an artists' paradise.

Opera Festival

The Opera Festival in Aix-en-Provence is the local highlight of the year, and as opera lovers we consider ourselves fortunate to be living here. The fun starts in early June when about three dozen young musicians arrive from all over the world for Master Classes—an honor they have won in an international competition. These master classes are open to the public and are a wonderful opportunity to see up close the hard work and the difficulty of the art of singing, cello playing, violin, piano, etc. Some of our past masters have included Isaac Stern for violin, Teresa Berganza for voice, and Pierre Boulez for percussion and conducting, but every year brings an interesting new crop. Some of the young singers may perform in the chorus of the operas to be performed in July, but all will give recitals and concerts in one or more of the lovely squares and courtyards in the old center of Aix in the evenings. A €15 "passport" gives access to all master classes and concerts during the month of June as well as to some dress rehearsals.

The serious excitement starts in July with the opening of the Opera Festival. Six operas are performed throughout the month in four different locations, and the city literally fills up with opera lovers. Hotels are full, as are restaurants and the terraces along the Cours Mirabeau—the Champs Elysées of Aix-en-Provence.

With a bit of luck you run into stars, but you don't need any luck to see famous faces in line at the various venues. I have made it a habit to have dinner at one of the two outdoor restaurants on the Place de l'Archeveché before the opera. With my tickets safely in my pocket, I can take my time to eat and watch the crowd gathering while I savor my dessert. I am sure to see current or former government ministers, well-known newscasters and other famous faces of politics and television, and even Gérard Depardieu with Carole Bouquet. Most of them have summer houses in the area and the air snaps with air kisses as they find each other and thrill at seeing and being seen.

Opera tickets go on sale in early February, and living steps away from the box office you might think that getting tickets is a cinch for us. Well, not quite. There are a limited number of inexpensive, subsidized tickets that sell out fast, and in hopes of getting any of these you have to get up early. Very early.[1] When Oscar got in line at 3:30 in the morning (the box office opens at 10:00 AM) he was number sixty-five in the queue, and when I replaced him at 7:00 AM the line curled around the block. I recognized a number of stalwarts from previous years and found the same convivial atmosphere of shared hardship in anticipation of our reward. Some people sat on little stools wrapped in blankets, others in heavy coats with woolen scarves halfway up their faces stamped their feet to keep warm, some read, others chatted. Snippets of family life floated on the still night air, and once in a while some lucky "liner" would be relieved by a mate and allowed to go home and to bed.

Surprisingly, people seem to be getting up earlier every year and this time there were two couples who had camped out all night with folding chairs and sleeping bags to be first in line the next morning. Perhaps not unusual for a rock concert but this is a crowd of retirees with many a grandmother among them. Tough little grandmothers who will wait stoically in the February night for seven to eight hours so that they can get tickets for themselves or a beloved grandchild at the affordable price of €28 (approx. $40). For those of us who buy everything, i.e.,

---

[1] Today some tickets are sold by telephone and Internet.

all six operas, these inexpensive tickets are manna from heaven.

Around 9:00 AM "breakfast" appeared in the form of trays of croissants and hot coffee, tea and orange juice, offered free of charge by the *Office de l'Opéra* to the chilled ticket line. It thawed the frozen crowd and sparked a palpable sense of excitement and anticipation. The end was in sight, the prize within reach, and the ordeal almost over. Another long night had been offered to the opera gods who would soon reward our devotion. Murmurs of "See you next year" were beginning to be heard and all of us bound for a night by our shared passion for opera were soon to disperse for another year. Perchance to meet again at one of the performances, where with a knowing wink we would proudly pat the "cheap" ticket in our pocket before finding our places among the expensive Orchestra seats. We can't suppress a secret feeling of superiority over all those who paid full price, before we sit down to enjoy Wagner's *Walkyrie* with Sir Simon Rattle and the Berlin Philharmonic (no less), or Mozart, Monteverdi, or Janacek. Forgotten the long wait in the chilly night. What long wait?!

Avignon 'Off'

What Aix-en-Provence is to opera, Avignon is to theater. During the month of July each has a festival and for one month Avignon becomes the theater capital of France. It is impressive enough to know that Avignon puts on over thirty "official" productions (*le festival "In"*), but the "unofficial" shows (referred to as "*le Off*") far outnumber the official program and have become to some the festival of choice. Take a look at these numbers for the "Off" festival of 2009: 825 companies put on 983 different shows in 105 permanent or temporary theaters during the sole month of July. Boggles the mind, doesn't it?

When Jean Vilar founded the *Festival Annuel d'Art Dramatique* in 1947, he could not have dreamed how immensely successful this event would become, attracting not only celebrated actors and directors to Avignon but also untold thousands of spectators from all over France and from neighboring countries. As always, the festival opens with a play by that year's "associate artist" performed in the imposing *Cour d'Honneur* of the Popes' Palace, and then spreads to the other theaters in town as well as to its cloisters, some churches, schools, and even an abandoned quarry. This première is often an exceptional event, for instance an 11-hour play by Wajdi Mouawad or a disturbing production by Belgium's controversial Jan Fabre, and may involve a big-name star. But let's take a look here at the less structured "Off" with its spontaneous combustion of youthful talent, energy and creativity, but with very little money.

The gamut of styles and subjects ranges from Greek drama to puppet shows, from Shakespeare to Schiller, from Molière to Marivaux to Oscar Wilde, from Sam Shepard to Amos Gitai and other contemporary writers, and many plays will have film, music and dance components as well. Shows start at 10 in the morning and continue throughout the day and evening, some in theaters of up to 300 seats but many more in smaller theaters of less than 100 seats. The catalog of "Off" performances is the size of a telephone book and can be consulted by author, location, theater company, and time table. Most of the "Off" plays last around one hour—some are as short as 45 minutes but none are longer than one hour and a half—and it is entirely feasible to see three plays in a day, as we often do.

For example, you can select a one-hour play that starts at 11:00 AM, after which you sit down to a leisurely two-hour lunch. You pick another play at 3:00 PM and a third one at 5:00 PM (all theaters are within walking distance) and afterwards find yourself comparing the relative merits of each show over a cool drink or an ice cream on a terrace under the platanes. If you don't want to stay around for dinner, you take the one-hour freeway drive back to Aix in time for the evening news and dinner at home. All in a day's work.

Of course, it is hard to tear yourself away from the street theater of Avignon where actors and actresses walk around in costume and stage make-up, handing out leaflets of their show to pedestrians and customers at café tables. "Come and see me at 6," they'll say, or "Last chance to see us at 8 tonight before we pack it in!" and so on, all with a pleading smile and perhaps a little dancing shuffle. Here comes a Dracula type with "blood" dripping from his chops who slips a blood-stained leaflet under my glass. And over there stands Don Quijote with a most unlikely looking horse, stoically waiting for Sancho Panza who has just accepted a proffered beer. There are musicians and dancers and masked harlequins from a *Commedia dell'Arte* group from Italy, and just as you think the show is over here comes a bearded bride with "her" bridesmaids and an unclear message.

All the world's a stage has never rung so true, and all the players here have earned their spurs by sheer versatility and dedication. These "Off" performers are more than actors; they have to do their own publicity, costumes, set design and sometimes even the writing of their show. They are the worker bees who turn this town into a crazy quilt of posters, pasted on boards or wrapped around lamp posts or tied to gates and parking meters. Not a single façade in the old center remains uncovered and the hapless tourist who wants to see the sights would do well to come back in August.

Of course, you will not see Jeanne Moreau or Isabelle Huppert doing this. They appear in the "In" productions at night at the biggest venues in town where you need to book well in advance. "Off" plays, on the other hand, rarely require reservations. Tickets to these shows are inexpensive and do not always cover the cost of the production. That is why an actor may ask you after a show to spread the word and send your friends, to sign the guest book, or to come and see him in another play at another theater. The best or the luckiest among them may get a contract or go on tour, some will get a favorable review in the press and a possible return engagement the next year, but all will have savored their taste of "Avignon" while it lasted and perhaps thought the thoughts that dreams are made of.

With this many productions there are bound to be hits and misses. I have seen some excellent plays here that were written and acted by outstanding young artists who are just one stroke of luck away from discovery and stardom. And I have seen others that had their amateurish slips showing. But it is safe to say that if you like the theater you will not be disappointed in Avignon, no matter where you go.

Most theaters have six to eight different shows a day running well into the night, and the streets won't empty until long after the last theater goes dark and the last diner has left the table. On your way to the car you notice new posters, or do they just look different under the street lights? You decide to check it out tomorrow when you return for another helping.

Sleeping Beauty No Longer

The attractions of Provence are many, but for the culture vultures among us Aix is particularly satisfying. This city of one hundred forty thousand inhabitants houses a large university, a conservatory of music, the French national dance center, an opera festival in summer, the only permanent Nô theater outside of Japan, numerous bookstores (one English-language bookstore where you can drink coffee or tea while browsing *The New Yorker*) and three multi-screen movie houses in the center of town (two of which show all movies in their original language with French subtitles), a municipal library which holds the manuscripts of Nobel-Prize winners Albert Camus and Saint-John Perse and contains an amphitheater and a movie theater for conferences, exhibits, and retrospectives of movie-makers such as Roberto Rossellini, Werner Fassbinder, Alfred Hitchcock, Michelangelo Antonioni, Akira Kurosawa, Gus van Sandt, Woody Allen and others.

The best thing the library organizes, however, is *La Fête du Livre* which takes place in October and features major writers during a three-day encounter. In the past ten years, we have had the pleasure to meet and hear there Philip Roth, Antonio Tabucchi, Toni

Morrison, V.S. Naipaul, and Russell Banks with Michael Ondaatje and half a dozen others whose work reflected "Une Autre Amérique"—a thought-provoking series of readings and discussions, punctuated by German actress Hannah Schygulla (think Fassbinder) reading a speech by Susan Sontag who was too sick to attend. [She has since died.] More recently, we have had Nobel-Prize winners Günther Grass, Kenzaburô Oé and Wole Soyinka, as well as Salman Rushdie.

Coming back to the Nô theater for a moment, it was very surprising to discover such a thing in Aix. This authentic Japanese wooden structure with open sides, built according to the very exacting rules of the art, is a gift to the city of Aix-en-Provence from Nô master Kano, a "living monument" in Japan. On two occasions several years apart I have been able to see Master Kano and other Japanese professionals perform the ancient art of Nô here with its magnificent costumes, masks and (to my ear) strange music, and with the help of a three-hour-long Introduction to Nô I am beginning to get the hang of it. Who would have thought that the city of Aix-en-Provence would hold the secret to this exotic form of art so very different from our own?

This cultural diversity keeps city dwellers like us happy and occupied, but foreign visitors need a wider spectrum and here our task as hosts is greatly facilitated by the proximity of a number of places of interest in the vicinity of Aix—such as Arles, Nîmes, Avignon, and Marseilles—that are well served by public transportation. A guidebook goes a long way to taking your visitors off your hands and gives them a chance to entertain you at dinnertime with their adventures and discoveries of the day.

For nature lovers, there are a number of treasures to be found within an hour's drive from Aix-en-Provence. A boat trip to the beautiful *calanques* in Cassis, for example, or the nearby Luberon mountain range dotted with attractive villages such as Lourmarin, Bonnieux, Ménerbes, and Lacoste where the Savannah College of Art and Design has established an outpost just below the chateau of the Marquis de Sade. Or, just a bit further, the marshy Camargue—a nature reservation known for its wild horses, its pink flamingos, its salt flats, and its birds—the antithesis of the flashy, crowded Riviera and, sadly, fighting for survival against the threats of global warming.

By the way, did you know that M.F.K. Fisher used to live on my street? Perhaps one more reason why I felt attracted to the place. In "Two Towns in Provence" she describes the years she spent in Aix-en-Provence, where she raised two daughters, and in Marseilles. And in a series of stories collected in a book entitled *As They Were* she even devotes a lengthy chapter to my street. She doesn't have much good to say about it, however, and complains bitterly about the noise. With her bedroom on the front of the house in this narrow street, she might still be bothered by night noise today, mostly coming from diners spilling from the two restaurants on this block. Gone, however, are the big garbage trucks of old that would collect and loudly crunch garbage (metal, glass, wooden crates and all) right under her window at dawn. Gone also are the sidewalks, replaced by stanchions to prevent illegal parking, and gone is much of the traffic that has found bigger and better roads around this narrow street.

But one of M.F.K. Fisher's "noises" that remains is the high-pitched whistling of the *martinets* (small swallows) at sundown as they whoosh by in our courtyard at incredible speed, wave after blurry wave, eating their body weight in insects in the process. It's a fascinating spectacle, lasting less than an hour, leaving you awed at the navigation system that allows such speed and precision without a crash.

Another seasonal "noise" may occur at festival time when students vacate their apartments for the summer and musicians rent them for a couple of months while they perform at the opera festival in Aix or the piano festival in nearby La Roque d'Anthéron. As you walk the city streets during June and July you are bound to hear some singer vocalize or a pianist limber up with rapid scales, and with a bit of luck you may be treated to an entire aria while you sip a drink at a café. I am sure M.F.K. Fisher would have liked it.

If at one time Aix was referred to as *La Belle Endormie* (Sleeping Beauty), she is wide awake today and endowed with everything her bigger sisters offer, especially when close neighbor Marseilles (France's second biggest city and a scant twenty miles away) is added to the mix. An international airport and a TGV railway station midway between Marseilles and Aix provide easy access. The sleeping beauty of Aix-en-Provence with her bourgeois refinement and the rugged longshoreman of Marseilles with his feet in the Mediterranean have given birth to a fine mix and an enviable quality of life along these ancient shores.

If in spite of that you still need a big-city fix now and then, you are only a three-hour train ride from Paris, a bit more than a four-hour drive from Turin, Italy, and some five hours' driving distance from Barcelona or Milan. All beautiful, all different, and all worth a visit before happily returning to the cozy bosom of Aix-en-Provence.

Râleurs

I once heard an "Italian" described as a "good-humored Frenchman" which made me smile and nod my head in recognition. The French are, and admit to being, *râleurs*—what we would call habitual complainers. It is a national character trait and applies to all levels of society. When I first settled here I was much impressed by the high standard of living: free education, low-cost high-quality health care for everyone, great public transportation, a 35-hour work week, retirement at age 60, long paid vacations, and so on. Coming from the free-market conditions of the United States I kept thinking how lucky these people are; some of the biggest worries of the average American citizen (affordable education and health care) do not even exist here! The French are truly blessed. So why are they complaining?

To understand this phenomenon we may need to backtrack a bit—say, to the end of the Second World War when many of the present-day social benefits were initiated or expanded. With the help of the Marshall Plan France was able to make a quick recovery and create lots of jobs. Like many other developed countries at the time, it began a period of uninterrupted growth that lasted more than 30 years *(les Trente Glorieuses—* roughly from 1945 to 1975)* until the oil crisis began to slow things down. During this time of expansion, which included a baby boom, the government extended many social benefits to its citizens who worked long hours and enjoyed full employment. Among these benefits was the right to paid vacation (which grew from a guaranteed two weeks in 1946 to five weeks in 1982), universal health coverage, generous family allowances, minimum wages, and numerous subsidies. The economy was booming and the country could well afford to be generous.

That is no longer the case and today the budget deficit seems to be the only thing that is still growing. The economy has slowed down, unemployment and deficits are rising, and Mother Providence at whose breast many French people suckle their entire lives is running out of milk. Since the end of World War II France has lost two wars (in Algeria and Indochina), saw industries decline, and the oil crisis as well as the more recent financial crisis have hit the treasury hard. The government can no longer afford its largesse and has begun to cut back on some of the generous benefits. However, today these benefits are considered *droits acquis* (acquired rights) and letting go of these rights is simply out of the question. The first post-war generation had known a life of increasing social benefits and the next one was born into a system of cradle-to-grave welfare, where what began as rights had grown into entitlements. The cycle had to be broken and the fight was on.

Today, that fight is played out on television and in the streets and continues to draw strong participation not only from labor unions but from professionals and public servants as well (doctors, lawyers, teachers) who march to defend their threatened workplaces and to object to further cutbacks. Amid a lot of noise and disruption attention is drawn to problems that may vary from the diminishing quality of public education to the price of milk, and in the end the dispute will be moved to the negotiating table where more often than not the protesters get at least part of what they were fighting for. It is the French way and people are not shy about loudly voicing their discontent. Children grow up with street demonstrations and strikes, and see their parents marching or supporting the strikers from the sidelines. It is generally believed that the government does not listen unless forced to do so by "the street."

An aside about "voicing their opinion." Have you ever heard a French debate on radio or on television? Frequently, everybody speaks at the same time and nobody listens. When I turn on my favorite radio news channel in the morning about five minutes early, chances are I catch a cacophony of voices "discussing" some issue where the first clear sentence is the closing one spoken by the monitor who thanks everyone for his contribution. At the end of the afternoon, a talking-head program on television offers the same spectacle: everybody around the table talks at the same time and the loudest voice or the longest breath usually wins. But I digress...

The *droits acquis* in France were awarded at a time of hardship and post-war penury, when they helped people get back on their feet and when the creation of a consumer society was a good and necessary thing for the citizen and the country as a whole. To the man in the street, these rights were acquired for life, and previous governments have paid the price for trying to take back some of those rights. Invariably, these attempts are met with fierce resistance and often the resisters win.

But with the well running dry and more going out of the nation's health care pot than coming in, some measures have already been taken to slow down the hemorrhage, such as the one-Euro out-of-pocket contribution to discourage unnecessary doctor's visits, reduced reimbursement for non-generic prescription drugs, more controls on habitual "sick leave" claimants, etc. But this is a drop in the bucket and more cutbacks do seem inevitable.

There is another French particularity that contributes to the tendency to resist: fear of change. The French are not risk takers; they know what they have and will instinctively resist something new. An inborn suspicion of losing something in the exchange easily results in the rejection of the new and different. I tend to think of this as a trait of older people, those who may not understand a newer world they cannot follow (computers, smartphones, etc.) and one they feel they do not need. But I have seen many highly educated youngsters here (Ph.D. level) taking *concours* after *concours* in hopes of entering the respected CNRS (*Centre National de la Recherche Scientifique*) for a poorly paid job with a lifetime guarantee. Here, job security definitely outweighs the more risky but financially more rewarding areas of business.

With a changing world, however, come perhaps more opportunities but also fewer guarantees, and the French are facing a future of less government assistance. It is scary and they are ill-prepared for it, so they massively resist it as long as they can. Both sides seem to have solid arguments and both will fight for their point of view until some common ground is found and an agreement is reached. The protest marchers will roll up their banners for a while, and the government will try to find the next area to cut without risking a revolution. Peace reigns, briefly, until the next battle.

It has to be said that protesters take to the streets to fight for more than their own purse (or their own "bifteck" as they say locally). For example, touch the Roma people, as president Sarkozy did when he began to expel them from France, and a spontaneous combustion of outrage spills into the streets where another march forms without prompting. Solidarity is part of the picture.

Perhaps the French are not more contrarian than others, but just more determined to hold on to their right to a decent life. Since they were given much they have a lot to lose, and being part of an increasingly competitive world they must realize that some of their *droits acquis* are under serious pressure. I see a long and noisy battle ahead, but this too will pass. In the meantime, they (and I) will continue to enjoy what is still an extraordinary quality of life in one of the most beautiful countries in the world.

Vive la Différence

It's been more than ten years since we left Washington, D.C. (doesn't *tempus fugit*?), and we increasingly feel at home in France but—boy—do things remain different here.

Take, for instance, this not uncommon sight in inner-city Aix-en-Provence: a parent walking with a little child suddenly steps into the middle of the narrow street to the shallow channel for rain runoff, takes the kid's pants down, then picks it up from behind in a sitting position and lifts it over the channel to do its *pipi*, puts the pants back on and steps back onto the narrow sidewalk with a gracious nod to the cars that have been forced to stop and wait for this little ritual. I have never heard a car honk and half expect that a driver who did so would get an earful from passersby. In the narrow one-way streets in the inner city, cars often have to wait for a truck to unload, or for a driver who stops at a bakery for a few baguettes, or for a youngster who honks at his friends who come running over to each give him the requisite number of kisses— so why not for a kid that has to pee? It's a damn sight cuter than the guy I saw the other day in a small nearby town where the N-7 cuts through. There, next to the one and only stoplight, this fellow took a pee against a tree in full view of a steady line of cars, shook his tweasel, zipped up and walked off without so much as a glance in the direction of his audience.

The very sexy advertisements are also different, especially a huge photo mural in the Paris metro, showing three panty-sniffing males, each holding a differently colored frilly little panty to his nose. Their expressions range from pleased recollection to close-eyed bliss, and seeing them bigger than life in several metro stations speaks worlds about the cultural difference of France. I dare you to imagine this in the Washington metro!

The kissing scene is interesting, too, particularly among the younger crowd who never pass each other without stopping for a number of kisses—anywhere from two to four. (I must make a study of this sometime; I believe the number depends on the region). You're sitting at a crowded sidewalk café, some teenagers approach, a "*Salut!*" is heard from behind and, like magnets, the two groups are drawn to each other, the walking teens squeezing through impossibly tight spaces to reach the sitting ones who turn up their cheeks to receive the expected air kisses, after which they all return to their respective conversations and destinations. Another standout feature of the young (and not so young) is hair color. I have seen colors here that don't belong to any spectrum: strange hues of red, green, blue, purple and sometimes all of them at once. Goes nicely with the popular fashion of *tatouage*, for both sexes, and varied hardware in numerous body parts.

Another difference is to be found on the beaches. Most Mediterranean beaches are relatively small, many are pebbled, but all are crowded in summer when it is easy to spot the new arrivals from the North. Their newly exposed bare breasts shine like headlights—high beams and low beams—among the tanned locals. Anyone, regardless of shape or age, can go topless and this draws no more attention than an exposed navel. The older women often wear more jewelry than cloth, and are always oiling or creaming their bodies, it seems, and touching up their hair. They look well-groomed, you might say, and seem totally oblivious to a missing piece of cover. Some men come off less well, especially when they are potbellied and wear a bikini-type bathing slip, standing in the surf (they don't seem to swim) with a cigarette stuck to their lip.

It is not unusual to find dogs in restaurants. They are generally accepted and usually no bother at all. But when dogs dine like people and sit on a chair it does get some attention. On a recent trip we spent the night at a hotel with a one-star restaurant where we decided to have dinner. Among our fellow diners was a couple with a poodle. Madame and poodle were seated on a banquette and Monsieur across the table facing them. They selected their menu and soon were served, all three, the same food on the same china. Poodle must have been there before because the waiter addressed him by his name, Maurice. After a while, it really did not seem odd, perhaps because Maurice was perfectly well behaved. He finished his plate without spilling and kept his paws off the table at all times. The only thing he did not do was take a sip of wine, but if he had woof-woofed nicely he might have been served that too.

But the greatest difference of all is the subject of food—a national craze if not an obsession. All commercial television and radio channels carry food programs, some of them aimed at children. Some school cafeteria cooks have begun to venture into *nouvelle cuisine* and try, within their fixed budgets, to guide youngsters toward acquiring adult tastes. In fact, every year in October there is a national *Semaine du Goût* which promotes the pleasure of eating as illustrated by chefs, restaurant owners, nutritionists, farmers and— why not?—the Minister of Agriculture himself. More than three hundred and fifty chefs fan out all over the country and hold "taste workshops" in public places and in schools, culminating in contests and prizes. The point of all this is not only to educate, but "*se faire plaisir.*" "Do yourself pleasure," says the website of an organization called the *Fraternal Cooks and Crafts from the Mouth*, "and put your buds awake!" We get their meaning...

In Other Words...

Few things give me more pleasure than language that is faulty but funny, by which I mean those pearls that drop from foreign mouths, mangled and bruised but miraculously conveying their intended meaning nevertheless.

Who could misunderstand: *"There are many ways to peel a cat..."*?

Or:

I have been empowdered to say...
Don't nurse a grouch (... hold a grudge)
What a potato couch!
He looks like such a bump
I screwed up regally
Smashed potatoes
What strikes your fantasy?
We are looking fast forward to seeing you again
It cost nothing—it was a frisbie
Let's play it by the ear
Birds of a feather think alike
We're not out of the blues yet
That situation is a tickling time bomb

These expressions lost none of their meaning but are bound to make you smile. Just like the immigrant handshaker who, with great formality and flourish, says: "How do you do it?"

During renovation work at our bank, management put up a little sign that read: "We ask our pleasant customers (*aimable clientèle*) to forgive the disturbance." No use asking the unpleasant customers, of course. And a charming little hotel in the old center of Aix-en-Provence promises "genuine furniture and extreme silence," while a welcome note in another hotel reads: "We hope you will be as pleasing as possible." Believe me, we will try.

An English-French sandwich board near a money exchange announces: "Purchase and Sale of Portion Currency in Rant Notes" which causes the perplexed tourist to consult the other side of the board with *Achat et Vente de Devises en Billets*. Why didn't you just say so?

Chateau de Beaupré, where we buy some of our wine, has upgraded its French brochure with an English translation that concludes: "Winegrowers and Owners, our wish is to preserve and introduce you to an Estate and we dedicate ourselves heatedly to this task which surrounds the admirable Beaupré Estate."

What does this have to do with Provence, you might ask? Nothing at all, I'm afraid, except that part of the pleasure of living abroad is the process of immersing yourself in a different culture, adopting a new lifestyle and learning a new language. If you understand the foregoing near-English you can be sure that the locals will understand your fractured French. It's the effort that counts and it's the effort that will be rewarded. The south of France is not Paris where, as in New York, people tend to hurry along and may be impatient with a struggling foreigner who needs time to get his French words all in a row. In Provence you have a good chance to be encouraged with a smile and helped along on your way to the full stop.

So if you plan to spend more than an occasional holiday here and perhaps settle in France, it is important to learn to speak the language if you don't want to be the perennial expatriate. Not only will it help you communicate with the locals and be accepted by them, but you are sure to be richly rewarded. It takes time and there will be moments of confusion along the way, but with a bit of luck and some good friends you will be waking up one day knowing that this is where you feel at home, where you fit in, and where somehow, at some imprecise point, you have become one of them. You have arrived.

Oscar's Recipes

Soupe au Pistou

Soupe au Pistou is a seasonal soup, made with ingredients found in the summer. It is important that the beans and the basil be fresh. Accompanied by a baguette or some good farmer's bread, this soup constitutes a healthy, solid meal without any fat.

[*Pesto* and *pistou* are similar but not the same. They may have similar origins that go back to Roman times—mixtures of garlic, herbs, and sea salt in olive oil—but pesto contains grated cheese and pine nuts while pistou only has the basic ingredients: fresh basil leaves, garlic, olive oil and sea salt.]

Ingredients for 6:

For the soup:

> 500 gr. (roughly 1 lb) fresh red beans in the pod
> 500 gr. fresh white beans in the pod (soaked dried beans are not a good substitute)
> 250 gr. fresh green beans (haricots verts)
> 2 medium white or yellow onions
> 4 very ripe tomatoes (or an 8-oz can of peeled tomatoes)
> 1 tablespoon of tomato paste
> 3 carrots
> 2 zucchini (if you follow the zucchini school)
> 250 gr. small dry elbow pasta
> 1 liter of vegetable broth (approx. 1/3 gallon)
> Olive oil, salt, pepper, a pinch of sugar

For the pistou:

> A whole plant of small-leaf basil (or 3 cups of large basil leaves)
> One large head of garlic or ten garlic cloves
> Olive oil, sea salt

Preparation:

Cover the bottom of a large pot with olive oil and simmer the finely-chopped onions until translucent. Add the red and white beans and the finely-diced carrots, and simmer for one or two minutes. Add the fresh tomatoes (previously peeled and chopped) or the canned ones and the broth. Add a pinch of sugar to neutralize the acidity of the tomatoes, if necessary. Simmer on a low fire until the beans are just soft (approx. 20 minutes).

While the soup is cooking, prepare the pistou as follows:

Put the garlic cloves and sea salt in a mortar (stone or ceramic are preferred) and grind them with the pestle into a puree. Add the basil leaves, a few at a time, and olive oil and grind them also, mixing them well with the garlic paste. Continue adding basil leaves and olive oil until you obtain a paste the consistency of mayonnaise.

Set aside half of the pistou in a bowl. Add the other half to the soup and add the dry pasta. Cook until the pasta is *al dente*. Some people like to add grated parmesan cheese at the end, but this is not "authentic."

Serve with bread and pass the bowl of pistou to those who want a stronger flavor.

Daube de Boeuf
(Beef Stew)

Ingredients for 6:

- 3 pounds of beef cut in large cubes. Cow's cheeks (*joues de boeuf*) are good, or any other tough cut of meat such as hind shank (*jarret*).
- 3 thick slices of smoked bacon
- 1 pig's foot or ½ calf's foot
- 4 large carrots thickly sliced
- 1 small onion studded with six cloves
- 2 coarsely sliced white onions
- 1 to 2 bottles of red wine. Côtes du Rhône or full-bodied wine is best.
- 1 8-oz. can of peeled tomatoes
- 1 tablespoon of tomato concentrate
- 12 black olives, pitted
- Condiments: 1 teaspoon thyme, 3 laurel leaves, some dried orange peel, 1 tablespoon red wine vinegar, one *bouquet garni*
- Olive oil, salt, pepper, flour, sugar
- One pound (500 gr. package) of dry large pasta

Preparation:

Put the beef, carrots, small clove-studded onion and the condiments in a large bowl and cover with red wine. Refrigerate, covered, overnight.

Take the meat cubes out of the marinade and pat them dry with paper towels. Lightly sprinkle them with flour. Cover the bottom of a large pot with olive oil and brown the beef cubes, a few at a time, on all sides. Handle the beef cubes carefully with tongs (do not pierce them with a fork), so that they retain all their juices. Set the browned cubes aside. Add the slices of bacon, each cut in three pieces, and the sliced onions. Cook until the onions become translucent.

Add to the pot the beef cubes, the pig or calf's foot, all the liquid of the marinade, and the remaining ingredients. Bring to a boil and immediately reduce the temperature to a minimum. Adjust the seasoning to taste and add a bit of sugar to counteract the acidity of the tomatoes, if necessary. Simmer very gently for seven to eight hours. After the first three hours, remove and set aside the bacon slices so that they do not become overcooked, and discard the orange peel and the laurel leaves. You may correct the thickness of the sauce by adding more red wine if too thick, or a tablespoon of flour dissolved in the cooking liquid if too thin.

Before serving, add the bacon slices, remove the bones of the pig or calf's foot and, using a sieve, remove the *bouquet garni* and the studded onion, leaving in the sauce only the beef, the bacon, the carrots and the pitted black olives.

Serve in deep dishes over a bed of large-size pasta or flat noodles cooked separately *al dente*.

Brandade de Morue
(Cod Fish Spread)

Cod is a fish of the Atlantic and the Pacific oceans. Dry salted cod was shipped from Portugal to the Caribbean to feed the plantation slaves, and it has become popular along the Mediterranean.

Fishmongers often carry two kinds of salted cod: the mildly salted kind that is less dry and only requires one or two days for desalting, and the traditional dry salted cod, stiff as a board, that takes at least three days to be desalted before cooking. Either of these kinds of salted cod is suitable to make *brandade de morue*.

As with so many traditional recipes, there are two schools for preparing brandade—with and without potatoes.

Preparation:

Start by desalting the fish. Soak it in the sink or in a large pot of cold water, changing the water frequently, for two to three days depending on the type of cod. Once desalted, put the cod in a large pot and cover it with water (or with milk) and gently boil it until it flakes easily with a fork (about 20 minutes). Drain it, let it cool, and puree it (in a mortar or a blender) together with as much garlic as you like, adding olive oil and milk (or, if preferred, some cream) until it has the consistency of a thick mayonnaise. Adding boiled potatoes helps achieve a creamy consistency (you may wish to experiment preparing *brandade* with and without potatoes).

Serve on slices of toasted bread or baguette, with a fresh rosé wine.

Epaule d'Agneau Confite
(Slowly-cooked Lamb Shoulder)

Generally speaking, lamb is a better meat here than beef, especially if it comes from Sisteron in the Haute Provence which is famous for raising the best lamb in the country. "Confit" is a different way of roasting lamb. After long hours of slow cooking in a very low oven the "confit" produces a very tasty tender meat that can be cut with a fork.

If you want to have it for dinner, start cooking at 10 AM.

Ingredients:

1 whole lamb shoulder with its bone
olive oil
Herbes de Provence
white wine

Preparation:

Place a whole untrimmed lamb shoulder (with bone) in a deep oven dish. Brush with olive oil and cover with Herbes de Provence (a mixture of thyme, marjoram, savory, and rosemary).

Place in a low oven — 120°C or 250°F — for 8 to 9 hours. Check from time to time and if there is no liquid in the bottom of the dish, add some white wine as necessary (it is important to always have some liquid in the dish). Do not turn over the shoulder.

Let it rest for 5 minutes before serving. Sprinkle with some salt when on the plate, not before. Accompany with vegetables and/or mashed potatoes.

Makes a wonderful leftover for lunch, at room temperature, accompanied with a green salad.

Foie Gras de Canard
(Duck Liver)

Foie gras (of duck or goose) is a standard feature in France during the Christmas-New Year season in all forms and preparations: canned, in glass jars, fresh, frozen or precooked. I prefer to prepare foie gras from scratch at home. This means starting the preparation at least three days before you intend to serve it. You need a porcelain terrine of about half a liter size to cook it in.

Get a whole fresh duck liver. If you buy it frozen, let it slowly defrost in the refrigerator during 24 hours. Then, with a very sharp knife take out the small blood vessels on the inside faces of the two lobes of the liver, being very careful not to damage the fragile flesh. Leaving some of the veins will not alter the taste, but they are rather unattractive. In frozen livers the blood vessels have usually already been removed.

Ingredients:

- 2 teaspoons of fine salt
- 1 teaspoon of white pepper
- ½ teaspoon nutmeg
- ½ teaspoon "Quatre Epices" (Four-Spices seasoning)
- 1 soup spoon of Cognac, Armagnac or Calvados
- 1 soup spoon of White Port

Preparation:

Fit the liver lobes loosely in a deep oven dish.

Put the salt, pepper, nutmeg and Quatre Epices in a bowl, mix them well and sprinkle the mixture evenly on all surfaces of the liver lobes.

Into the same bowl mix the cognac (or armagnac or calvados) and white port, and pour the mixture over the lobes, turning them so that they are wet all over.

Cover the dish with cellophane and place it in the refrigerator for three days.

Then, take the liver out of the deep dish and move it to the terrine as follows:

> Very gently press the liver lobes, the smaller one first and the larger covering it, into the terrine, trying to leave no empty spaces. Be careful not to break or damage the flesh.

> Cover the terrine with its top, place it in a large pot, with hot water covering two thirds of the terrine, inside the oven preheated to 300°F (150°C). Cook *à bain Marie* for 35 minutes.

> Let the terrine cool and then place it in the refrigerator for 24 hours before serving.

Cut in thick slices and serve with toasted bread.

You may accompany it with a fig chutney or with fresh figs.

Serve with a sweet white wine; a Sauterne if possible, or a Beaume de Venise.

Magret de Canard
(Duck Breast)

Duck breast is an extremely flavorful meat that is very simple to cook. It requires no sauces or condiments, only a bit of patience. One magret serves about four people.

Preparation:

Put a heavy skillet on a low fire and place the magret fatty side down in the middle of the pan. After 5 or 6 minutes the bottom of the pan will be filled with liquid grease.

Holding the magret down with a wooden spoon or other utensil, carefully tip the pan and pour the liquid grease into an empty can or wide-mouthed glass jar.

Continue to cook the magret slowly and to pour off the liquid grease into the jar every so often. You will notice after a while that the magret contracts and becomes rounder and darker in color but the top continues to be cold to the touch.

After about 40 minutes, you will notice that the amount of liquid grease begins to decrease. Check the bottom of the magret to see how much grease is still left. If the remaining grease is only a couple of millimeters thick and well browned, turn over the magret and cook the top part for 5 minutes.

Serve immediately, cutting the magret in slices about 1 centimeter thick. It is often accompanied by ratatouille.

[The duck grease that you collected in the jar will solidify once cooled. It will keep well in the refrigerator and is excellent for making risotto.]

Pissaladière

Pissaladière (from pis salat = salted fish) is a white pizza popular on the French Mediterranean coast, topped with sautéed onions, anchovies and black olives. Traditionally, the crust is made with white-flour pizza dough, but I prefer a lighter variation and use pâte feuilletée (puff pastry dough) instead. Normally a number of anchovy filets decorate this pizza but instead I like to put a thin coating of anchovy paste underneath the onions. This is entirely optional, of course.

Ingredients:

2 lbs white onions
1 small jar of mild anchovy paste or,
if not available,
8 anchovies to top an 8-portion *pissaladière*
black unpitted olives

Preparation:

Peel and thinly slice 2 pounds of white or yellow onions. (You may also use frozen sliced onions).

Cover the bottom of a heavy skillet with olive oil and gently cook the onions at low heat, turning them from time to time, until they become caramelized. They will have reduced in size by more than half and should have become light brown in color. They will taste sweet. Let them cool for a good while.

Preheat a 400°F oven. Place a round puff pastry sheet on oven-proof paper in a pizza mold or on a cookie sheet if your puff pastry sheet is square. Cover it, except for a ½-inch border, with a very thin layer of anchovy paste. Add the caramelized onions. Decorate with a few black olives that you unpit yourself—they taste better than the commercially available pitted ones.

Bake until pastry is well browned, about 20 minutes.

Serve as a starter course or as a snack to accompany drinks.

Ratatouille

Nothing better to accompany meat, especially lamb, in Provence than ratatouille, a flavorful vegetable stew traditionally cooked slowly overnight on a hot stove and eaten the next day. It can be served as a light lunch, and as a leftover it can also be added to pasta.

Ingredients for 6:

2 Eggplants
2 Sweet peppers (one green, one red)
2 White or yellow onions (large)
2 Courgettes (zucchini)
1 Large can of tomatoes or 4 very ripe tomatoes
(optional additional ingredient: one or two celery sticks)
Olive oil
Salt, pepper
Herbes de Provence

Preparation:

Cut all vegetables into small cubes.

Cover the bottom of a large heavy pot with olive oil. When the oil is hot, simmer all the vegetables simultaneously for about 20 minutes on medium to low heat until the eggplant is soft. Add the *Herbes de Provence* and gently stir the vegetables, making sure that they remain moist. If necessary, add a bit of warm water.

Add salt and pepper to taste. Serve lukewarm.

P.S. Ratatouille is very similar to a Sicilian dish called *Caponata*. See the next page.

Caponata

This traditional dish from Sicily resembles the French "ratatouille" but without the zucchini. Caponata contains the ratatouille ingredients of eggplants, peppers, onions and tomatoes, but in addition it has vinegar, capers and black olives.

Ingredients for 6:

- 2 Eggplants
- 2 Sweet peppers (1 green, 1 red)
- 2 White or yellow onions (large)
- 1 Large can of tomatoes or 4 very ripe tomatoes
- Olive oil
- Salt, pepper
- Wine vinegar (1 teaspoon)
- Capers (in vinegar – 1 teaspoon)
- 12 pitted black olives
- (optional additional condiments: some pine nuts and seedless raisins)

Preparation:

Cut all vegetables into small cubes, and prepare like ratatouille in a heavy pot. After adding salt and pepper to taste, gently stir in the capers and vinegar plus the optional condiments if desired.

Serve at room temperature or cold but not refrigerated. Accompanies meat or fish dishes.

Risotto

Even though Risotto is an Italian dish, it is quite popular in France and appears on many restaurant menus. Our French friends seem to like it but we have our disagreements about some of the ingredients. The traditional recipe (which I follow) requires Arborio rice and the Italian dried mushrooms called *funghi porcini*. With a certain French rebellion our friends often use common rice and dried French mushrooms (*cèpes séchés*) swearing they are exactly the same as *funghi porcini*.

Ingredients for 6:

- 1 small white onion, chopped
- 6 demitasses (half tea cups) of arborio or carnaroli Italian rice (other rice does not work well for risotto)
- 4 cups approx. of bouillon (vegetable or beef)
- ½ cup of dried mushrooms (*funghi porcini*), cut in small pieces and soaked in hot water (use other dried mushrooms if you cannot get porcini). Mushrooms can be substituted by almost anything: asparagus tips, tuna, etc.

Saffron, salt, pepper

½ cup approx. of grated parmesan cheese

- 2 tablespoons approx. of olive oil

¼ cup of Sherry wine or white vermouth

- 1 tablespoon of butter

Preparation:

In a medium-size heavy pot, fry the onions in the olive oil until translucent. Add the rice and continue to cook over medium heat 2–3 minutes until the rice is well coated with oil and starts to become a bit translucent, stirring constantly with a wooden spoon.

Add the sherry or white vermouth and continue stirring until the rice absorbs the liquid.

Start adding the bouillon ½ cup at a time and continue stirring. As the rice absorbs the liquid continue adding more bouillon, stirring slowly all the time.

Once the rice grains become larger (approx. 10 minutes from the start) add the mushrooms with the water in which they were macerated. As the rice absorbs the liquid, continue adding more bouillon, stirring slowly all the time until the rice has become al dente (approx. 20 minutes from the start).

Add the saffron dissolved in some bouillon, and the butter and enough bouillon to make the risotto creamy. Turn the heat off and let it stand for 5 minutes, uncovered, before serving.

Just before serving, add ½ cup of grated cheese and more butter if necessary to keep the risotto soft and creamy.

Serve in warmed soup plates adding a bit more grated Parmesan as decoration.

Socca or Panisse

Socca, as it is called in Nice, or Panisse, as the slightly thicker version is called in Marseilles, is a flat pie or thick pancake made with chickpea flour which is popular along the Mediterranean and in North African countries.

To add to the linguistic confusion, it is also known as Farinata in Genoa, Italy, where it is said to have originated, and as Fainá in Argentina where Italian immigrants introduced it. The Fainá I remember from the Argentine River Plate was professionally cooked in wood-burning pizza ovens in large round very shallow pie molds.

The Socca you find at take-out places in France is made by mixing chickpea flour with water and olive oil, and frying the resulting paste in a hot skillet until well browned on both sides, but with a soft moist center.

For preparation at home, I prefer to use the oven.

Ingredients:

>   3 ounces chickpea flour
>   1 ounce white wheat flour
>   13 fl oz water
>   1 tablespoon olive oil
>   Salt, white pepper.

Preparation:

Put both types of flour in a bowl and mix gently while adding water little by little. This should result in a very smooth, liquidy batter.

Add the oil and salt to taste and mix it with a whisk. Let the mixture rest at least two hours, stirring it from time to time.

Preheat the oven to 450°F.

Cover the bottom of an 11-inch pie mold with olive oil and pour in the liquid batter. The batter should fill the mold to a depth of about ½ inch.

Bake for at least 30 minutes or until the pie is golden brown. (During the baking process the pie will first become inflated and will then flatten again before beginning to brown).

Serve at room temperature after sprinkling lightly with white ground pepper.

This can be served as a starter course or, when cut into smaller pieces and eaten with toothpicks, as an accompaniment with drinks before dinner.

Torta Pasqualina
(Spinach Pie)

This spinach pie from Genoa is traditionally prepared during Lent but I use it any time of the year. It is a more substantial, thicker pie than the French "tartes salées" and as such a nice variation on the theme of "tartes" as a first course.

Ingredients:

> 2 sheets of *millefeuille* dough (puff pastry)
> 1 onion finely chopped
> 2 or 3 garlic cloves finely chopped
> 2 lbs frozen or fresh spinach leaves grossly chopped
> 1 cup grated Parmesan cheese
> 4 eggs
> 1 teaspoon Maïzena
> 4 slices of white bread cut into small cubes softened with a bit of milk
> Salt, pepper and a generous sprinkling of nutmeg
> Olive oïl

Preparation:

In a large wok or frying pan put some olive oil and let the chopped onion and garlic cook for a little while. Add the chopped spinach little by little until wilted if fresh, or thawed if frozen. The total amount resulting should be about 4 cups. Let it cool off.

In a large bowl mix one egg, the Maizena and the bread. Add the spinach and the condiments (salt, pepper and nutmeg) and gently mix. Taste the mixture and adjust the seasoning if necessary.

Butter the inside of a bread mold or line it with baking paper. Put one of the dough sheets in the mold leaving a generous border to overlap. Fill the mold with the spinach mixture. Using your finger make two holes in the spinach mixture and put one raw egg in each hole (they will become boiled eggs once the pie is cooked). Cover with the second sheet of dough and after cutting off the excess, moisten the edges with water and curl them together forming a cord on the four sides of the mold.

Beat the last egg and with a brush paint the top of the preparation (to give it a nice color when baked).

Bake in 450°F oven for about 40 minutes or until the crust becomes nicely golden-brown. Let it cool and remove from the mold.

Serve at room temperature as a first course.

Tarte aux Figues

Figs are plentiful in Provence, with two summer harvests (usually late June and late August), and because fig trees do not require much care or pruning they are very common in provençal gardens. In fact, friends who have fig trees will often give you home-made *confiture de figues* because ripe figs will not keep well and need to be eaten within a day or two or be preserved as jam or chutney. Of course, figs are also available at our daily farmers' markets and I like to buy the very ripe blue figs to make a fig pie. It is a naturally sweet fruit that requires no added sugar and is extremely easy to make.

Ingredients:

- Fresh very ripe figs (blue or green), soft to the touch and fragrant
- Puff pastry – either a round or a square sheet to fit a pie mold with a 1-inch standing edge
- Buy enough figs to cover your pastry sheet with tightly packed halved figs, the cut side facing up.

Preheat your oven to 430°F and bake your pie for about 20 minutes or until nicely browned.

Serve it lukewarm with a scoop of vanilla ice-cream.

If ripe figs are not picked they will fall off the tree and either be eaten by birds or rot away. But you can collect these figs on a shallow tray, cover them with thin gauze to keep the flies off, and leave them to dry in the sun. They'll shrink and wrinkle a bit in the process and become an intensely flavored delicious snack that keeps all summer.

Apple-Fig Pie

Those figs that are too damaged to top your pie can be used for making jam or simply cooked down to a soft spread that I sometimes use on an apple pie. There is no need to add anything but a touch of sugar in boiling these figs; you simply cook them briefly to eliminate moisture and thicken them a bit.

The resulting mushy spread adds an interesting touch to an apple pie. It's best to use rather sweet apples (like Golden Delicious).

Place a puff pastry sheet in a round pie mold and spread a thin layer of fig paste onto the dough. Peel your apples and slice them in thin moon-shaped slices. Arrange these, slightly overlapping each other, on the pastry sheet starting on the outside rim. Sometimes I brush on a bit of apricot glaze, but this is optional.

Bake at 430°F for about 20 minutes, like above. Once the pie has cooled you may want to slice one or two fresh figs, lengthwise, to decorate the pie.

P.S. If you reduce the figs a bit more, let's say to the consistency of a firm paste, this can make a delicious accompaniment to *foie gras*.

Acknowledgment

Thank you, Oscar, for your infinite patience and your computer expertise—of considerable help in the preparation of this book. And, of course, for your cooking: the gift that keeps on giving.

CPSIA information can be obtained at www.ICGtesting.com
Printed in the USA
BVOW02s2345220215

388841BV00001B/29/P